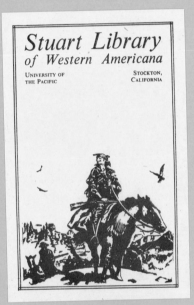

TULITAS OF TORREÓN

THE WULFF FAMILY IN THE GARDEN OF THE WULFF HOME IN SAN ANTONIO

From left to right: Dalla Wulff, Fidi Wulff, Harry Wulff, a friend, Carolina Wulff Tyrrasche, Linda Tyrrasche, Junie Mayer, Paulita Wulff Lammers, Fred Wulff (Papa), Helena Wulff Mayer holding Amy Mayer, Triny Wulff, Alice Wulff on Linda Groos Wulff's lap (Mama), Max Mayer, Lula Wulff, a maid, Anita Tyrrasche, Marguerite Mayer, Maria Wulff, a friend, George Mayer.

TULITAS OF TORREÓN

Reminiscences of Life in Mexico

by

TULITAS JAMIESON

as told to

EVELYN PAYNE

❧

TEXAS WESTERN PRESS

The University of Texas at El Paso

1969

COPYRIGHT 1969

TEXAS WESTERN PRESS

Library of Congress Catalog Card No. 69-20291

For Susie and Jim,

Bill and Lynn,

who are the future

CHAPTERS

PHOTOGRAPHS

PROLOGUE

W WHEN PAPA, ARMED with degrees in civil engineering and architecture from the University of Hanover in Germany, returned to his native city of San Antonio, Texas, in 1876, he was at once made city engineer — or words to that effect. He built a number of bridges over the meandering San Antonio River (one or two are still in existence) and attended to other municipal chores. He also had his eyes opened to the depths to which man can fall, such as too much sand in the cement and similar chicaneries, and he finally resigned in righteous indignation. The scope for civil engineers in that part of the country being more or less confined to the job he had just quitted, he was forced to take his talents and training elsewhere. He went to New York, armed with letters of recommendation from all the prominent citizens of San Antonio, including his father, the park commissioner, and his father-in-law, the banker, and accompanied by his wife and baby son Fidi.

The metropolis was not impressed with Fred Wulff. Many of the men to whom he applied for work had never heard of San Antonio, let alone its local bigwigs, and, furthermore, there were lots of engineers floating around. Before he finally succeeded in getting a job as a draftsman, Papa had been reduced to putting cardboard in his shoes and inking the fraying creases of his trousers.

The firm was a good one, and he made progress there, but the stipend was small. When he had first graduated from college he had been sent to Mexico to build a dam for a big

PAPA (FEDERICO WULFF) *photographed in San Antonio, Texas when he was 30 years old.*

firm, and now unexpectedly he received another offer from them to go back to Mexico and build another dam. The opportunity seemed too good to pass up, especially since the family had been augmented by one (me) in the interval.

Robert Louis Stevenson once wrote a story which is three tales in one. In it, if I remember rightly, a knight starts on a journey — he has a choice of three roads to take. Stevenson wrote three accounts of what happened, and the result in every case was the same — he got knocked on the head or something equally fatal. I suppose the author was trying to prove that it didn't matter much which route you took — you wound up the same way eventually. But, then, death isn't the important thing — it's what you do with the time in between. Papa's decision to go to Mexico really changed our lives.

I sometimes wonder what would have happened if he had stayed in New York. We would have grown up to the tune of *Take Me Out to the Ball Game* instead of *La Paloma;* we would have watched baseball instead of bullfights. Skyscrapers, Wall Street, Vanderbilts and Tammany in lieu of Porfirio Díaz, *enchiladas* and revolution. Education would have been right at our doorstep — grade school, high school and college in the neighborhood instead of having to be provided by governesses or tutors, or sought for, just as expensively, in the states. Our way of living would have been straightforward and in line with that of the rest of the community instead of an uneasy compromise between the rigid and formal Mexican customs and our own laxer ones. Our accents might have been Manhattan or Bronx instead of a sort of hodgepodge of three tongues. Who knows — we might even have gotten rich, for the firm Papa had been with later became large and well known. As it was, just about the time Papa was getting on his feet financially, with one son in college and fair prospects for educating the other three, the Mexican Revolution began and the bottom fell out of our lives, economically. If we had stayed on in New York, we might have held out till 1929!

But the years in Mexico gave our lives a very distinct flavor, compounded of many things, an intimate acquaintance with a variety of other nationalities, a first-hand look at a totally different society, the ability to talk and think in three languages. Papa and Mama were both part German, and Mexico was full of Germans, so that although we were still very much Americans (perhaps more so, as one's nationality always seems to be emphasized in a foreign country), the sauerkraut took its place right alongside the tamales and the ham and eggs.

It was a life full of variety, not only of incident but of personalities, a continuing shortage of money, and an awful lot of fun. Looking back, I wouldn't have missed it for anything.

Chapter I — SAN ANTONIO

❧ I WASN'T QUITE TWO when we moved to Mexico, and as I had suffered a good deal from colds and bronchitis in the dampness of New York, Mama and Papa lived in a tent for awhile in order to cure me up. Papa built his dam and landed some other commissions for bridges and things, sending down the roots that would bind us all forever to the country in some fashion or other. They seem to have moved around quite a bit in the area, for Harry, two years younger than I, was born in San Pedro, and Alice came along three years later in Lerdo. Those were both established towns and, for that particular part of Mexico, fairly good sized. Torreón, where we finally settled, was just a-borning. In fact, one of Papa's earliest commissions was to lay out the town. (Fifty years later Torreón was the fourth largest city in Mexico, and they had a grand anniversary celebration and presented Papa with a scroll or certificate as father to the place.)

Here too we had our first Christmas tree. Papa made it by boring holes in a broomstick and sticking in branches of greasewood, which must have looked rather strange with the delicate German ornaments — the glass birds with the spunglass tails — and the candles. But of course we children thought it exquisite.

Shortly after that, when I was four and Fidi five, Papa decided it was time we had some education. He was influenced no doubt by the fact that while both of us were fluent in Spanish and German, neither of us spoke any English. So Mama packed up the four of us children and went to San

Antonio, where she and Papa had been born and had grown up.

I had not been particularly aware of my surroundings in Mexico, but the contrast was a vivid one. To see so many trees — all around, growing wild. (In Torreon nothing grew wild except cactus and mesquite and greasewood.) And the houses, so wide open and inviting with yards full of grass and shrubbery and flowers, not all drawn inside themselves like the Mexican ones. Everything was so green, green, green! There were even, wonderful to say, paved streets, some with wooden blocks, some with cobblestones. And so many, many people!

Mama rented a house down near King William Street in the section called Sauerkraut Bend, and we were surrounded by relatives, both sides of the family having been exceedingly prolific. They were all surprisingly congenial too.

Mama and her four sisters and their cousins — thirteen girls in all — had grown up together, and the friendship continued down through the years, involving husbands and in-laws and offspring. They were mostly plump comfortable women, good-hearted and conscientious, beautifully unaware of any connection between high-blood pressure, arteriosclerosis and similar ailments and the ingestion of large amounts of rich food. (Everyone knew things like that ran in families!) So they cooked, not in any sterile, vitamin-conscious fashion, but in a mouth-watering, terribly fattening way to please the palate. The purpose of eating was to acquire nourishment, and the tastier the food, the greater the nourishment (and the fun). A recipe calling for a whole pound of butter was bound to be better than one requiring only a half pound. Margarine and other synthetics had not been born, but if they had, I'm sure Mama and her family wouldn't have touched them with any length pole. If you didn't own a Jersey cow, you took milk from someone who did. Cream that had to be spooned from the pitcher was normal everyday fare. I don't know where the milk went to — we children didn't drink it. They used lots of sugar and honey and pecans, since Texas grows lots of pecans, and they were all Texan to the bone (or should I say the kernel?). There were cakes so light that they had to be held down with inch-thick icings, rolls that vanished in your mouth like a puff of smoke, great roasts of beef with thick delicious gravy, chickens cooked in a dozen delicious ways, home-made bread that tasted better than any bakery ever smelled, *tortes* smothered in whipped cream . . . Even the humble cabbage was transformed into manna when stuffed with ham and eggs and served with quantities of brown butter sauce.

There was always plenty of help to be had in San Antonio — German, Polish, Bohemian girls from the country, who were big-boned, amiable and thorough. They lived in small hot bedrooms on the second or third floors of the big stone or brick houses, using brooms and wet tea leaves for sweeping, washboards and yellow soap for laundering, and scrub brushes. They generally stayed until some strong, silent farmer scraped up courage enough to propose. Then they went back to the country to raise dozens of children and live thrifty, hard-working lives, while a new generation of Annas and Gretchens took their turn at the kitchens.

No matter how well the girl learned to cook or how long she stayed, Mama never left her unsupervised. None of this "there'll be twelve for dinner tonight, James" stuff. Mama was always on hand to oversee every detail of the cooking and serving. Sometimes it was quite a dilemma — whether to be with one's guests and run the risk of some dire occurrence, such as the *kaffee kuchen* being less than piping hot, or to neglect the guests and see to the food. One woman Mama knew solved the problem nicely by putting her chair in the doorway between dining room and kitchen so she could keep an eye on the food and an ear on the gossip at the same time.

Mama and her sisters and cousins met once a week for a *kaffee klatsch*. Franz, one of the male cousins, christened it the Run It Up and Run It Down Club. Each hostess tried to outdo the others, and the big round mahogany or walnut tables creaked under the load of cakes, cookies, rolls, *tortes*, and so on. The ladies always set to with gusto and the conversation would run something like this:

"Oh, Linda, your rolls are always so marvelous. I just wish I could get mine as light as yours."

"Oh, you're sweet to say so, Lottie, but I don't think they turned out so well this time. The oven must have been too hot."

"Your gold cake, Linda, is the most delicious I've ever tasted. You gave me your recipe, but I just haven't your touch — mine is never as good as this."

"Oh, Anchen, nothing can compare with your cakes. Besides, this seems a little heavy — it must have fallen."

And so on, with the guests praising the food, and the hostess, flushed and deprecating, running it down.

While this was going on Fidi and I were going to the old German English School, which our grandfathers had helped to found. I have no recollection of what I studied or learned there, although it must have been appreciable, since the school was run with German thoroughness. My only memory is of the annual recitation day, when the desks were freshly varnished and the whole place decorated with ropes of laurel. Nor do I recall what Fidi and I might have contributed to these occasions, although Mama, like all the other parents, was certainly on hand to flush with pride or squirm with embarrassment. There was always food and drink afterwards at one of the relatives' houses by way of celebration.

Most of the male kindred considered themselves connoisseurs of wine and beer, which were served in even the most abstemious households. Hard liquor was usually confined to occasions that were strictly stag and to bars, of which San Antonio certainly had its share. One of the favorite haunts was the old Buckeye Saloon, for a time one of the town's most prized tourist spots.

Much more clear in my memory are the things we did after school. Granpa Groos, Mama's father, was handsome and stern and prolific. Mama's mother bore him eight children, and after she died he remarried and fathered eight more. The youngest members of the second family were about our age, and we played together, frequently going to the big house, built of the yellowish Texas granite. It was on Commerce Street, a huge affair, the entrance hall being big enough to hold a dance in. We had a regular ritual to go through. First there was food, naturally. Granpa Groos's austerity did not extend to his table. There were two excellent German girls, and every day was baking day. Sometimes there were great slices of watermelon, or peaches or grapes or other fruits in addition to the cakes and cookies. When we had stuffed ourselves full we each took a turn at riding the old neck-breaker bicycle — one of those with the big front wheel. That little seat was a terrifyingly long way from the ground, but no exceptions were permitted. After that we dashed under the house where a number of hens were always stubbornly sitting on eggs. We dragged out the poor old clucks and doused them with water. Maybe they weren't supposed to hatch the eggs — at any rate, no one ever interfered with this sadistic sport. After that we were free to play as we liked, or rather, as Fidi liked. He was the leader and the rest of us followed, scared or not, walking fences, jumping off roofs and so on.

The only exception to this tyranny was when Ida, my best friend, and I played dolls. How we loved those dolls and how we suffered for their sakes! Fidi and Ida's brother, Jimmy, were close friends and, in the manner of older brothers, incorrigible teases. Ida and I were usually the targets, especially when we wanted to play dolls. We finally took refuge in an old outside bathroom. It had not been used for years, but there was still a reminiscent odor, and it had a galvanized iron roof. There, with the door locked and the windows shut and the sun beating down, we were safe from everything except heat stroke.

On Sundays sometimes Granpa Groos would take Mama and us out for a ride in his fine carriage with two beautiful horses, and we would usually end up at a park where they had soda pop and great big pretzels.

Papa's side of the family offered just as much entertainment. He was the eldest of nine, so some of the youngest were still young enough not to be classed as too adult in our minds. They were all thin and blue-eyed and full of energy. They were talented mimics too, artistically and musically gifted. One of them, Uncle Henry, was a fine sculptor. Granpa Wulff had a great stone house that looked like a castle and was set in a huge garden. There were brick-rimmed walks with geraniums set all along the sides, and a goldfish pool filled with water hyacinths. His place stretched back to the river, a distance of several blocks, and there were boats, a boathouse built on floating barrels, and a wonderful place to swim. His office was directly under the tower of the castle, and there we usually found him, a kind, jolly man with a big black cigar invariably between his lips. He always asked if we had been good, and when we said yes (sometimes with fingers crossed behind our backs) he would open one of the drawers of the big roll-top desk and produce long strings of licorice, cutting off pieces for us with a pair of scissors.

Next door lived the Mayers. Tante Helena was Papa's oldest sister, married to fat, jolly Uncle Max. The older children were about our age, lively, gifted and full of the devil. We had lots of fun with them and not infrequently got into trouble. One of our favorite pastimes was trying to shock poor Uncle Henry, who was, despite popular notions about sculptors, fearfully strait-laced and surprisingly innocent.

We lived in San Antonio for five years, and as far as we children were concerned, we could have continued living there indefinitely, even though we missed Papa. But Mama and Papa were tired of living apart and finally decided that they would have to try tutors or governesses.

The rented house was given up, and Mama must have gone through prodigies of shopping, for we had to take along enough for the whole family for a year — clothes, linens, kitchen utensils, medicines and everything else. Among other items, sixty pairs of shoes. Not too many actually for a family of seven for a year, but certainly more new shoes than either Fidi or I had ever seen all together. We were given the engaging task of scratching up the soles, so we wouldn't have to pay duty on them, and we set to work with gusto, but before we finished even our destructive instincts were so well sated that we had to be nagged into completing the job.

The last two weeks before our departure we spent with Tante Lit, one of Mama's sisters, and her husband, Uncle Nep Ronse. They were both very kind people, very patient, and we had, of course, visited them before. But they were childless, and we had never been there so long or in such numbers. I'm sure they were relieved, although they never hinted at such a thing, when the great day arrived. We and our luggage were stuffed into two hacks, the good-byes were said, and we started for the station. Tante Lit and Uncle Nep promptly collapsed, but not for long. In an hour we were back, having missed the train.

Chapter II — BACK TO MEXICO

W FIDI PROBABLY really did look forward to the move back to Mexico — he was a boy and adventurous, and he may have found our San Antonio household rather overrun with women. Harry, the next brother, always took his cue from Fidi. And, of course, there was a certain prestige and excitement about being a potential world traveler. But I didn't anticipate it with any pleasure. I was a fearful, anxious child (all my early pictures show me apparently on the verge of tears), and Ida and I wept at parting, and I was quite sure that no one would ever replace her and that I would be forever lonely.

I'd sort of forgotten what riding on a train was like, but it began to come back to me as soon as I smelled the smoke, and some of my qualms diminished. (People who have never ridden behind a coal-burning engine don't know what they have missed — from a nostalgic point of view there is no fragrance like it.) The noisy puffing of the engine, the occasional frightening bursts of steam, the novelty of looking through a dirty window at a swiftly vanishing landscape. At Eagle Pass we had to change trains, and we found ourselves with many more Spanish-speaking companions, who were excitable and voluble and carried all sorts of odd luggage, but otherwise there was little difference between the American and Mexican railway systems. There was the enthralling business of watching the porter make up the berths, the grown-up sensation I had as I climbed the ladder into the upper and pulled the green curtains shut. Just like being in

{8}

a little house of my own, with the additional charm of speeding along in the darkness. I finally fell asleep through sheer weariness, but each time the train jerked to a halt I woke and listened and wished I had a window to look out of. Or someone to talk to, for Alice was sound asleep alongside me, rolled into a ball, and none of my pokings and whisperings did a bit of good. So I lay and listened to the porter moving about and people getting on and off and talking in subdued voices. Outside there were other sounds, some quite incomprehensible, until the train pulled itself together again with a good deal of noise and went on its way.

There were other items of interest, the water cooler, for example. We made endless trips back and forth, to the annoyance of some of the other passengers, and Mama tried feebly to stop us, but she always suffered badly from car sickness and lay back against the scratchy green plush, looking wan and ill. About all she had energy for was Bub, the youngest, who was still in diapers. Then there was the rest room, which was a little terrifying, especially in the early morning when it was full of women in wrappers and kid curlers. Open suitcases were spread out all over everywhere, and the ladies, nearly all stout and wearing long laced-up corsets and fancy corset covers, combed their long hair, stuffing in rats and switches and endless quantities of hairpins. When the train lurched they begged each other's pardon in acid tones, and from time to time one would pick up her suitcase and claw her way past the green curtain and out into the car. Alice and I scampered around in the dark corners under the washbasin and the long board that served as dressing table, investigated the faucets and the hair receiver and washed ourselves gingerly while Mama struggled with Bub.

At first it was rather exciting to eat picnic style off our laps. But then the sandwiches began to get dry and tasteless and tiresome, and we whimpered for something different and more appetizing. We didn't get it, though, because the train carried no diner, and even if it had, I'm sure that Mama would not have felt herself capable, either emotionally or financially, of dealing with five children there.

With the advent of so many Mexican travelers the whole tempo of the trip had changed—conversations were lengthier, shriller, and accompanied by many gestures. At every station some of the passengers would eagerly buy things from the vendors who swarmed around the stations — things to eat, which smelled perfectly wonderful, such as *tortas compuestas, tamales,* oranges and so on. Mama wouldn't buy us any of those either, probably feeling that our insides would be safer and more comfortable with the known edibles we had brought along.

Our first sight of Torreón was not encouraging, except as a termination to the now tedious train ride. The terrain was dusty and sand colored, almost bare of vegetation. Only Fidi got any kick out of it and that mostly by speculating as to whether there might be any snakes and what other wild animals we might expect to encounter. But there were mountains, something the rolling San Antonio country did not offer. There were several ranges, with the blue-gray peaks fitting between other peaks like parts of a puzzle. Mama, in answer to our repeated questions, wearily promised that we would be taken on a mountain-climbing expedition right away, and that helped relieve our disappointment.

Papa was at the station to meet us, along with practically the entire population of the town, since the advent of the daily train was part of the show. We weren't particularly interested in the foreigners, who looked just like people every place else, but the Mexicans were worth staring at. San Antonio had had a lot of Mexicans, but these were so much *more* Mexican. The men wore white trousers and shirts, with the tails hanging out, sandals *(huaraches)* on their feet, and large straw or felt *sombreros* on their dark heads. Some wore leather aprons with a number on them. These were the *cargadores*, the porters licensed by the government, and they lifted Saratoga trunks and mountains of suitcases without any sign of strain, although they were mostly smaller than the men we were used to seeing. I might add that the *cargadores* were extremely trustworthy, and I don't recall ever hearing of anyone losing anything through their ministrations.

The women were nearly all swathed in black shawls (*rebozos*) and generally looked shapeless and depressing. The *rebozo* is a larger and hardier version of the *mantilla* and can be wrapped in such a way that it makes a pouch for parcels or even babies. The long fringed ends make good dusters or fly whisks. Altogether a versatile and useful garment. But it was the children we really looked at. Enviously, comparing our high shoes with their cool bare feet (crusted with dirt and horny with use), our high-necked, long-sleeved clothing with their brief, thin garments. The very youngest ones wore nothing but a tiny shirt reaching to the navel (no diapers), and I wondered whether Bub, squirming in all the stuff they put on American babies at that period, realized what he was missing.

We piled into a couple of *coches* and drove along the unpaved dusty streets, bumping over a string of railroad tracks that went straight through the middle of town. Freight trains sat on them, puffing or entirely quiescent, while people walked around the cars or even, sometimes, crept over the couplings between them. Beyond the tracks we could see a mountain, a sandy, barren upshoot which seemed to be right in the middle of town too. It was actually nothing but a good-sized hill, and years later Papa was to build a great gray stone house on its slope and even later Villa was to take his guns to the summit and shoot down at the town.

Torreón was then very small and centered around the railroad station. As a matter of fact, if there had been no railways, there would have been no town. The mountains all around were full of useful metals, and under the welcoming aegis of Porfirio Díaz foreigners were rushing to tear these metals from the earth. And other people naturally were rushing in to provide services and goods. Torreón lies in the center of the Laguna district, an immensely fertile stretch of desert which was once a big lake. When we lived down there, some of the old men could remember the lake before it dried up and vanished. Alongside the town is the Río Nazas, the so-called Mexican Nile, which is bone dry nine months of the year and a raging torrent the other three. By means of irrigation, cotton, wheat and other crops were grown and very profitably too.

The place was quite a little melting pot — there were English, French, Germans, Canadians, Americans, Spaniards, Chinese, Arabs, Swiss and several other nationalities. Thinking back, it occurs to me that it was rather like a frosted two-layer cake. The layers were the Mexicans, high class and low. The frosting was of foreigners, and the filling, meagre enough, consisted of those foreigners (principally Germans) who had married Mexicans and managed to combine both cultures. Perhaps because the foreigners were few and usually stuck together, you always managed, no matter where you went in Mexico, to encounter someone you knew or had heard of or who was related by blood or business ties to someone else you knew. It gave a small-town flavor to the whole country, and strangers were generally welcome, especially if they happened to be of your own nationality. There were times, of course, when you were left with a bad check or a bad taste in the mouth, but on the whole it turned out pretty well.

The houses were adobe, generally stuccoed in various pastel shades, with long barred windows and tall narrow doors. The door-knobs were, for some reason, always set too close to the jamb, so that you pinched your fingers, and the keys turned the wrong way. The houses came right to the edge of the brick sidewalks or the dusty streets with neither porch nor yard, seeming to huddle together in fear or contempt. The patio was in the middle of the house, an oasis of loveliness, full of plants and vines, lovingly tended and invariably yielding the maximum of color and scent. Behind the house was the corral (or perhaps two corrals) for the livestock. Sandwiched between the houses were the stores and saloons and offices, for until very recently Mexican towns seldom had "residential districts." There was the plaza, a small moth-eaten park, with benches to sit on and, later on, a tinny-looking bandstand. Across from the plaza was the church, which was pale green with large chocolate spots where the stucco had washed away.

The house Papa had rented was on Viesca Street and at the very edge of town. Twice a day, night and morning, the herds of goats and cattle going to pasture swept by us, adding a couple of layers of dust each time. The house was typically Mexican with thick walls, a door and a narrow barred window facing the street, a patio, and the corral in the rear. The front door was stout enough to withstand a battering ram, and it opened into the *zaguán*, which was a wide hall with a tile floor, flanked on one side by the *sala*, on the other by the dining room. The rooms were all very high ceilinged, long and narrow, and by virtue of the sparsity of windows, rather dark. The ceilings were covered with *manta* (unbleached domestic) stretched tight. We were seldom conscious of the ceiling cloths except during rainstorms when the roof leaked— we never had one that didn't. Then the *manta* would develop an ominous swelling, which reminded you uncomfortably of Kipling's "The Recrudescence of Imlay" until one of the servants took a long pointed stick and poked a hole in the cloth to let out the accumulated water.

The *zaguán* farther on debouched into a big patio, around which were the other rooms. The patio was full of plants, some set in the ground, others in undisguised lard cans, and they flourished beyond belief, for the Mexicans all love flowers and they all have green, green thumbs. Way in the back was the corral, which harbored two Jersey cows and a flock of chickens. It was surrounded by an adobe wall six feet high, broken in the middle by a high curbed well, which we shared with the house immediately behind us, the Hotel Madrid.

Early in the morning everything was closed up tight, shades or drapes pulled shut, and the high ceilings and thick walls kept the house cool. Theoretically, the same treatment was supposed to keep the house warm in winter by holding the heat in. It didn't work that way, possibly because we never accumulated enough heat to hang onto. The heaters were *braseros*, small iron boxes big enough to hold half a dozen sticks of wood. It was rather like trying to light a cathedral with a birthday candle, but that was long before the days of central heating and we weren't spoiled. We wore long underwear and lots of outer wear, and since the homes of our Mexican friends were always infinitely colder (they considered it unhealthy to heat a house), we got used to it. Besides, the winters were short and not severe.

There were six servants — the *mozo*, the cook, and four maids, all very pleasant, if not always too efficient. The cook was fat and middle-aged, with no teeth in front and her graying hair screwed into a knot on top of her head. She looked about a thousand but was probably only in her late forties. Two of the maids were elderly, but the others were young and pretty. They wore their hair in long braids which were looped across their shoulders and tied at the ends with minute pieces of red or green ribbon. The *mozo*, about whom more later, was short and coffee colored, with beautiful white teeth, very thick black hair, wearing the white cotton trousers and shirt that nearly all of them wore. The women all wore gold hoops through their earlobes — the ear piercing was customary and considered very beneficial to the eyesight.

When we had gotten ourselves settled we washed our hands and faces at the bowls in our rooms and trooped into the dining room to eat. The meal was long and strange, beginning with soup out of a tureen and going through half a dozen courses, the next to last being Mexican beans, *frijoles,* which had been boiled, mashed and fried. This was invariable, not only at our house, but everywhere else. The dessert was peculiar too, being *cajeta de membrillo* (quince paste). All sorts of fruits were made into *cajetas,* which were small hard loaves of the paste, and one served thin slices of the stuff. Other desserts were *flan* (plain baked custard) and occasionally sherbet. There was another sort of *cajeta* which we adored — *cajeta de celaya, jamoncillo,* or simply *leche quemada,* which means burnt milk. Milk and sugar are cooked together for a long time until the mixture is thick and sticky and delicious. It was sold in little round wooden boxes and eaten messily with a spoon. The taste is that of a considerably intensified version of Borden's Eagle Brand, out of which, incidentally, you can make it without much trouble. There were oranges, small but sweet, limes instead of lemons, mangos, which were marvelous once you got used to the tinge of turpentine in the flavor.

Nowadays mangos are sold in the United States and even canned, but for the benefit of those who have not yet encountered them, I should explain that they are orange colored and the shape and size of a very large egg, a turkey egg, perhaps. In the center is a big seed, to which the orange meat clings tightly. You take a mango fork, which has two short tines outside and one long one in the middle and plunge it deeply into the seed. Then if you are grown up or are trying to be on your best behavior, you peel it and cut the meat off daintily with a knife. Otherwise you simply eat as you would around an apple core. The difference being that mangos are *very* juicy, and the only really satisfactory way to eat one is stark naked in the bathtub.

There were also the native dishes, some of which we had tasted in San Antonio. Nearly all of them were flavored with onion, tomato, chile, either red or green, and often garlic. We all took to them, even Bub, like ducks to water. We loved the *tortillas,* either flour or corn, the *gorditas* (meaning little fat ones) which are made of the same *masa,* a kind of corn-meal paste, that the *tortillas* are made of. *Tamales* are also made of the *masa.* I could go on indefinitely about Mexican food, which is delicious, particularly the soups, but I won't. Not now, anyway.

After the meal came the *siesta,* which was not entirely an alien experience because in San Antonio during the warm weather most people took a short rest in the afternoon. But it was nothing like as comprehensive as the Mexican version. The entire community stopped short — stores and businesses closed, and the only people out and about were the "ladies of the evening," who were permitted to ply their dubious trade at that time. And, of course, their customers.

The *siesta* lasted a good two hours, and then we had some much-needed baths. The bathroom was a small room containing only a large tin tub set on legs, which was filled by the servants with tubs and tubs of water. It had a plug in the bottom, but the water simply emptied into other tubs to be carried outside and thrown out. The bedrooms all had wash-bowls and pitchers for in-between use, and the rest of the plumbing was situated in a small wooden house in the corral. We immediately discovered that the door to this, which was secured by a plain old hook, would, if hit in just the right spot, let go and swing wide. From then on it was standard, whenever any of the other children was in there, to hit the door and run. (Once, unfortunately, our intelligence service failed us and the door flew open to expose the stoutest and most dignified of the aunts.)

Clean and rested, we went into the *sala* to find Mama and Papa. He did his best to answer all our questions and promised that we would climb a mountain first thing next morning. Then unexpectedly he and Mama went over to the piano to play duets. They both played well and enjoyed it. But we didn't — not right then, anyway. We were alone in a strange country, an alien land, and our parents, who should have been supporting us through the transition, were paying no attention to us at all. They were playing stupid old duets and obviously thinking only about each other. I never felt so forlorn in my life, and I could see on the other children's faces the same expression I felt on my own. I resented Papa then passionately for diverting Mama's attention. In San Antonio he had been only a visitor, very welcome, but set down in the midst of our accustomed environment. Here he was different — the environment was his, and he was usurping not only Mama's authority, but her attention too. In short, for the first time in our lives we were seeing our parents not just as convenient extensions of ourselves, but as people in their own right.

Chapter III — FRIENDS

◍ THE AWFUL MOMENT PASSED. One of the servants, perhaps sensing our discomfort, mentioned that there were some children living in the house behind us, and we all rushed out to see. Climbing on boxes we peered over the corral fence into the corral of the Hotel Madrid, which was run by a family of Spaniards. There were several children, dark haired, dark-eyed and about our age. We greeted them in English and then in Spanish, and they just put their thumbs in their mouths and stared at us. We tried all sorts of things, but we couldn't get a word out of them. Finally Fidi said, "I know. The masks."

Among the few treasures we had been allowed to bring along were two masks, just ordinary black ones, and Harry ran to get them. Fidi called after him, "Bring both of them."

One of the little Spaniards echoed, "Boze a dem."

We felt cheered and christened them the "Bosians" on the spot, but even with Fidi and Harry grimacing and gesticulating with the masks on we made no further progress. Not another word could we get from the children, and we consoled ourselves by chasing the chickens around the corral until one of the servants came out and put a stop to that.

The next morning we went mountain climbing, starting very early in the morning in order to get back in time for breakfast. It was cool and delicious with a lemon-colored sky and the dust settled for the moment. We just climbed the hill beyond the tracks, but no Alpine explorer ever got any more satisfaction out of his experience than we did. It

FEDERICO WULFF *in his office in Torreón*

Mexicans building a rolling cylinder dam

Bridge on Johnson Street, San Antonio, built in 1880 by Federico Wulff

TULITAS *(Dalla) at age 7*
Picture taken in San Antonio in 1893.

FREDERICK *(Fidi) 8 years old*
Photograph made while the
family lived in San Antonio so
the children could attend school.

was exciting to see the town diminishing, to watch the ant-like people coming out of their tiny houses and to see miniature trains puffing along. I kept a sharp lookout for snakes and wild animals, remembering Fidi's speculations of the day before, but we encountered nothing more lethal than cactus. There were also dusty-looking clumps of mesquite which in San Antonio grew to tree height but here were only scraggly bushes. We saw lizards, a rabbit or two, and many rocks and much dirt. A very satisfactory expedition to everyone except Mama, who looked at our feet and sighed. We had to leave behind our old shoes in order to save space in the trunks, and the climb had effectively ruined three pair of shoes.

With the easy adaptability of children we were soon settled in our new home, speaking Spanish with facility, getting used to having six servants instead of one "girl," and growing accustomed to the strange climate, architecture and habits. For the first few days we had no one else to play with, and perhaps this welded us into a tight group, for although Ida and I had hidden from the boys in San Antonio in order to play dolls, in Torreón my dolls gathered dust while I followed Fidi's lead.

He had a fertile imagination and he was, as Alice said, the "bosser" of us all. We did as he commanded. Lots of times my heart was in my mouth when I had to climb fences or jump off high places, but I never hesitated. And, looking back in this safety-conscious age, at the things we did, the risks we ran without anyone ever saying a word or paying much attention, I wonder how we did it. Our guardian angels must have been on the job twenty-four hours a day. The youngest child always had a *nana* (nurse) but the rest of us were more or less under Fidi's care except when it was time for meals or baths or school. And since he was certainly not yet ten when we moved back to Torreón, it must have been a pretty heavy load for him to carry, despite the rather autocratic power he wielded.

In the patio Papa had had a *volantín*, a sort of foot-power merry-go-round, installed. It was just two boards crossed on a swivel, and you had to wind a rope around the center post and jerk, as you do with a top, in order to get it started. We lay on the boards on our stomachs and pushed with our feet till it was going at top speed. Then we hung on, tooth and toenail, pushing whenever it slowed even slightly. Perhaps it was considered sissy to get off — at any rate we stayed till we were too weak and dizzy to hang on any longer. Then we fell, rolling as fast as possible out of the way of the others' feet and those flying boards and lay on the ground till we got our breath and sense back. Then we climbed on again. The patio, incidentally, had been planted to grass, but it never grew despite the servants' best efforts, for the *volantín* never stopped. It was the only one in town, and there was always a line of children waiting.

Out in the corral Papa put up a tent for us. We probably played many different games, but what I remember best was the circus. Fidi, of course, was the ringmaster and cracked his whip with a flourish while the rest of us obeyed orders. I was the bareback rider, standing gracefully on old Jack's back for as much as five seconds at a time.

Jack was one of the ponies Papa bought us. Jack was old and tired and had to be beaten into a trot. Billy, the other one, was younger and sprier. About that time Papa was building a dam near Torreón, and now and then as a special treat Fidi and I were allowed to ride out with him early in the morning to the site and have breakfast there with the laborers. Coffee was made in a big tub, very strong and black, with the peculiar flavor of what was called *caracolillo* — that is, the wizened or stunted beans. We drank it Mexican style with a great deal of hot milk, and with it we ate *frijoles* and *gorditas de harina* and, naturally, *tortillas*. At home we had to use forks, but out there we could roll up our *tortillas* as the peons did and use them to scoop up the beans and chile, biting off a piece of *tortilla* with each mouthful. Nothing ever tasted as good, nor did anything smell as wonderful as the smoke from the burning mesquite roots mingled with the fragrance of the coffee.

Somewhat later, just about when Papa was finishing with the dam, Billy, the pony, went berserk one day. He dashed into the patio from the corral, chewed up everything edible and kicked everything else to bits. Jack by that time was developing some of the difficulties of old age, so Papa got rid of both of them. We didn't really miss them very much, for by that time we had scraped acquaintance with the Bosians and some other children.

As I said, the well in the corral wall was shared by us and the owners of the Hotel Madrid. About a week after our arrival one of our chickens flew up and fell into the well. In the ensuing excitement the ice was broken and thereafter the Bosians were our dear friends. There were four of them, about a year apart, making a companion apiece for us. They came and rode on the *volantín*, played in the tent and with our toys, while we found their corral, cluttered with boxes and trash, a fascinating spot.

There were the Perry children, too, who lived a few houses away and were numerous and fun. They had a pet *chivito*, a baby goat, and great was the excitement when it somehow managed to leap into their privy. We all rushed over and watched with bated breath while the men tore up the seat and rescued the poor creature.

Right across the street lived the Severin family. There were four children, and Mr. Severin made soap out of cottonseed. Their yard had a great pile of cottonseed hulls, and we spent hours clambering to the top of it and sliding down. Why we—and the Severins—survived, heaven knows, for the stuff was as slippery as sand, and periodically one of the younger children would disappear into it altogether. Luckily, we bigger ones always managed to fish them out before they smothered. Another inducement to visit their house was provided by the big oven in their kitchen. Like most foreigners, they had, in addition to the regular wood stove, *braseros* for the servants to cook their own food on, and this oven had been built into the wall for the servants' use also. It was big enough for us to hide in and spring out at the unwary souls who wandered in.

There were other playmates who lived at a greater distance and when we played at their homes the *mozo* was always delegated to take us to and from. Nowadays it would be unthinkable to entrust a child to someone about whom we knew as little as we did about some of our *mozos*, but nothing ever happened to us, nor did I ever hear of anything happening to anyone else's children. Kidnaping did not come into style until the Revolution.

Alice, five years younger than I, was the only one of us to challenge Fidi's rather absolute rule. She was plump and muscular, a tomboy, and afraid of nothing. Since she was good-natured and usually ready for anything, she generally went along with the rest, but now and then she'd disagree and if he threatened her, she'd stand with arms akimbo and say defiantly, "Do me something." She made a little garden for herself in one corner of the patio and put up a little sign: "Nobody Dass Go into Alice Wulff's Garden."

My best friend was Kika Pfeiffer, just my age. She lived clear across town, beyond the tracks and up on the side of a hill, where her father had a soap factory. (I don't know how the town's economy supported two soap factories, especially when such a large segment of the population eschewed the product so completely, so perhaps I am mistaken about Mr. Pfeiffer. Anyway, whatever he did had something to do with cottonseed, for I distinctly recall the rather cheesy smell which pervaded the place.) Kika was blonde and plump and altogether delightful, and we always had a wonderful time together, especially when I went to her house to play. The only fly in the ointment was that Kika's sister was just Alice's age, so I always had to take Alice along. Alice must have been the original beatnik, for she hated clothes, hated things touching her. Mama made most of our dresses, and Alice was her biggest headache, for no sooner had Mama pinned the front of the dress together when fitting it than Alice took a deep impatient breath and popped all the pins out. The strings of her high shoes were always hanging in loops and they were never tied. She rolled her black cotton stockings down to the shoe tops and rolled up the legs of the long underwear. When she appeared like that I always protested vigorously at having to take along such an untidy creature and Mama would come out, hairbrush in hand, to see that Alice made herself presentable. But the improvements never lasted long, and as soon as we reached the Pfeiffers Kika, whose sentiments about younger sisters coincided with mine, and I would run away and hide. Alice, as always, enjoyed herself hugely and seldom wanted to leave when the *mozo* came to get us. Once, in fact, she refused to, and after bringing me home, he was sent to drag her back, still protesting.

Next to the Hotel Madrid and directly behind our house was Papa's brewery. After one trip through it we stayed away, both because we had been forbidden to go there and, more important, because we were afraid of the brewmaster, who was a gigantic German with a temper to match. But behind the brewery and very accessible was an enormous coal pile where we spent a great deal of time — all our time, judging by the way we usually looked. One of the brewery's by-products was a stream of boiling water, perfectly clean, and Papa built a little brick-lined ditch to bring it into our patio where it flowed into a shallow basin and from there under the *zaguán* and out into the street in front. It was very handy, for we could dip out hot water at all times for bathing, cleaning, cooking and washing. We children used to float little boats in it, and Bub, the youngest, when he was still not yet three, one day fell head first into the basin. Fortunately he was wearing a *vichol* (a cheap straw sombrero with a round instead of a peaked crown), which slipped down and protected his face and neck until he could be fished out. As I said, our guardian angels were really exceptional.

It was a very gay and carefree life, for with six servants, we were never called upon to do any chores, and once school was over we could do as we liked. One morning this pattern of happiness was spoiled. When we went out to the corral and looked over the fence we saw Jesús, the oldest of the Bosians, sitting there crying. When we asked what the matter was he looked up, his big brown eyes magnified enormously by the tears that kept welling up and running down his brown cheeks.

"María is very sick," he explained, hiccuping. "Very sick. She—she might even die."

We simply stared at him. Death we had heard of — in San Antonio a relative or two had died. There had been tears and black clothes and funerals, but it had been remote. We had seen one or two funeral processions—the black horses and plumes and the hearse and carriages full of mourners. In Torreón death had come closer. The town was so small, the sandy desolate cemetery close by, and death was so much more frequent. Nearly every day we saw one of the pitful little processions—men carrying the coffin followed by a doleful straggle of black-garbed men, women and children. Once in a while there was a black-painted wagon and some following *coches*, but usually the procession was on foot. Far too often the coffins were very small, small enough to be carried on a man's shoulder. And now, we realized, they might soon be carrying María that way.

Worried and afraid, we ran in to tell Mama. She shook her head and as soon as possible she went over to the Hotel Madrid. When she returned, looking depressed, she tried to explain to us and comfort us. Later on we heard her telling Papa, "Poor little thing. The doctors have given her up. And, it's really gruesome, Fritz, but you know how they are. The aunt went down and bought a bolt of black cloth, and she and the mother are already busy making mourning for the whole family."

Mourning at that time was pretty elaborate everywhere, but in Mexico it was really something. There was a rigid and detailed code, giving the exact number of days of mourning prescribed for every degree of relationship, even the most distant cousins, and for friends. Widows frequently wore black for life; those who could afford it had black underclothes, and even children wore it a year or two if a parent or sibling died. One girl of thirteen I knew was in black for three years, first for her father and then for a series of relatives. Every house had black veils and armbands, for even a call on a bereaved friend called for mourning clothes. So that Mrs. Bosian's activities, although they struck us as a trifle ghoulish, were quite in keeping with prevailing custom.

In the middle of all this María unexpectedly and inexplicably began to get well. But thrifty Mrs. Bosian sewed right on, and María is probably the only person in the world to have worn her own mourning.

Chapter IV — SCHOOL DAYS

✿ OUR FIRST GOVERNESS was a Fraulein somebody or other, who came very well recommended by a family in Mexico City. She was middle-aged or more so, homely and arch, and she seems to have functioned both as governess and housekeeper, for I remember that she carried a great bunch of keys hung by a ribbon from her waist, and she waved her long crooked forefinger at us all over the house. She wore mob caps decorated with multitudes of little bows and bits of lace. She had dozens of them and she was always sending to Germany for ribbon and things to make more. Rumor said she was minus most or all of her hair, and naturally we children were wild with curiosity. Certainly she never had such attentive and interested pupils, for we followed her about, praying for a high wind or a darting eagle to snatch the cap off, and in the schoolroom we kept our eyes riveted on her head. Even Alice, who had to be found every morning and propelled (with a hairbrush) into the schoolroom, appeared voluntarily during Fraulein's regime.

There was no bedroom for Fraulein, so one end of the huge schoolroom had been partitioned off with *manta* walls (rather like stage flats) complete with door and lock. However, the ceiling was so high that it had not been thought necessary to take the walls all the way up, and we spent half our time standing on wobbly piles of furniture to peer over the top, still hoping to catch her without the ever-present cap. But we never did — she must have slept in it too.

There was such a shortage of women in Torreón and so many lonely foreigners that any single woman not actually

bedridden was immediately beset by hordes of suitors. Fraulein was no exception — a stout German widower soon took
her out of circulation, caps and all.

Papa then advertised in a New York paper. He was either
a genius at ad-writing or the market for governesses was very
bad, because he received 400 replies. Just how he decided
on Mrs. Carling I don't know, but no doubt he was influenced
by the fact that she was a widow and close to forty. But she
was also, despite her graying hair, rather pretty, and inside
of a week nearly every man in town or in the immediate
vicinity was paying court to her. So importunate were her
beaux that she took to fobbing us off on the Schmidt's governess, who either had halitosis or was a man-hater. Papa had
paid Mrs. Carling's fare from New York and she was getting
a good salary, so he was understandably annoyed. Especially
since the popular hour for calling coincided with the time at
which the *mozo* milked our two Jersey cows. When he came
through the patio with two buckets of what was virtually
pure cream, the suitors (mostly living in boarding houses or
mining camps) began to drool audibly. Papa was too hospitable to turn them down. He was also too good-natured to
scold Mrs. Carling, but even his patience was wearing thin.
No telling what might have happened if she had waited any
longer to make up her mind which one to marry.

Discouraged with women, Papa decided to try tutors. Several were imported at considerable expense and were immediately weaned away by offers of higher salaries as clerks
in stores or mining camps. Then came Herr Rausnicht, who
was a dapper little man, nattily dressed. His mustache was
waxed and twisted into a work of art, and his collars — well,
he sent to Germany for them, there being none in the western
hemisphere high enough and stiff enough to suit him. He
had a peculiar mincing gait, his right arm moving rhythmic-
ally across his stomach while his left hand, clutching a fine
malacca cane, sawed across the small of his back. Every

morning we all hid behind the big front door, and as he went down the hall we lined up and followed, mimicking him exactly. Oddly enough, he never caught onto this, or if he did, he considered it a compliment. I don't think he taught us very much, and, anyway, he didn't last long. He began staying away to celebrate birthdays — the Kaiser's, Porfirio Díaz's, Queen Victoria's, since a great friend of his was an Englishman, and, since we were Americans, President McKinley's. Invariably Herr Rausnicht celebrated with such zeal that he had to take off the following day to recuperate. Papa put up with this for awhile, hoping he would get the birthdays out of his system. After all, even heads of state can only have one a year. But when Herr Rausnicht sent word that he was staying away to celebrate his own birthday, that was too much. Papa fired him.

I don't know what happened to Herr Rausnicht, but we always suspected that he went back to Germany to give Wilhelm II lessons in mustache twisting. At any rate, Papa didn't hire any more tutors, for by that time a small school had been started by a Mr. Langer. I don't know how many pupils there were or whether our usual playmates attended, for the only other child I can recall there was a little German boy named Fritzi. I don't remember what or how Mr. Langer taught us, but no one could possibly forget his disciplinary methods, which were both unique and practical.

The school was held in a typical Mexican house with barred windows and a patio. In the patio was an arbor loaded with grapevines, which seemed to be unusually fruitful. Either Mr. Langer could not or would not hire someone to pick them, so for minor offenses we were sent out to pick grapes, so many bunches for each dereliction, and woe to the child who succumbed and ate even one grape. The grapes were purple and juicy, and it was impossible to get by with eating even one. The patio also harbored an inexhaustible nest of large red ants, and grape-eaters and other flagrant offenders were told to bring in so many dead ants. The schoolmaster counted them too. Alice was a tomboy who appeared constitutionally unable to conform to his ideas of how a little girl should behave, and she spent most of her time at the ant bed. Every afternoon when we got home from school Mama would ask, "Where's Alice?" and the reply invariably was, "Killing ants."

Mama must have thought she needed the discipline or else she and Papa went on the theory that the teacher was always right. Anyway, no one ever stepped in to criticize his methods. Of course, when the grapes gave out we all had to kill ants — in that climate they were a year-round pest. One night when we were walking around town we passed the school and saw Fritzi's tear-stained countenance peering unhappily through the barred window. He had been sent out to kill ants and Mr. Langer had forgotten all about him and locked him in.

Later on a Mrs. Somebody and her sister, Miss Burton, started another school, about which I recall only one incident. We were having some sort of school festival, with the pupils giving recitations and generally showing off. In the middle of everything the principal announced, "And now Miss Burton will step up and get married."

Groom and minister were produced and the ceremony took place on the spot. I never found out the why of this — I can only surmise that Miss Burton preferred being married in her natural habitat.

Scholastically we didn't seem to suffer too much from this varied educational diet, for when Fidi and I returned to San Antonio we were up with, if not ahead of, our American-schooled contemporaries. I don't know why, for none of our teachers made any real impression on us. Except, possibly, Fraulein. For years whenever we saw her stout husband, grown much stouter on her excellent cooking, we stared at him wistfully, wishing we dared ask what he had found under those caps.

Chapter V — MEXICAN MORES

✿ ONE OF THE MOST SERIOUS obstacles to understanding between Americans and Mexicans lay in the fact that the United States was a nation of middle-class people. The very rich and the very poor were, comparatively speaking, negligible in both numbers and impact. Moreover, status in the United States was not fixed — any boy could get to be President or compete with the Vanderbilts. In Mexico, on the other hand, a small group of very rich people not only ran the country but owned, literally, better than ninety per cent of it, and the chances of a peon getting very far up the financial or political ladder were practically nil. This led many Americans (and some other foreigners too) into looking down on the Mexicans, rich and poor. Many a woman who had never had anything but a hired girl who ate with the family found it very heady to be able to employ half a dozen servants for $15 a month.

Mexicans neither understood nor accepted the American's hustle and bustle, the feeling that things should be done on time, that appointments should be kept, obligations met, and so on, and the Americans were continually exasperated by the Mexicans' indolence, procrastination, and general laissez-faire ways. I have heard this indolence explained on the basis of the excess vitamin B resulting from the eating of so much chile, but on the whole it seems more likely that it is simply the result of generations who tilled their little plots of ground, getting almost enough to eat sometimes, and the lack of ambition developed from learning by experience that no matter what they did they weren't going to get any further anyway.

There were other things, of course — language was one. Another lay in the matter of courtesy. The manners of all Mexicans, down to the smallest child, were exquisite. Charles Macomb Flandrau in his *Viva Mexico,* which deals with the same period, said that if he had the ordering of this world, all children would be born Mexican and stay that way till they were fifteen. All this had nothing to do with morals or ethics, just manners. Even the poorest peon would say, "My house is yours" and use similar flowery phrases, which to us sounded fantastic and insincere, while they, of course, considered us blunt and crude. The real difficulty, I suppose, lay in the basic concept of politeness. The Mexican said whatever he thought it would please his audience to hear, and it needed to have no basis in fact nor was it supposed to be taken literally. American politeness was less effusive, and "Sincerely yours" certainly sounded more genuine than "I kiss your hands and feet," which was often used at the end of a Spanish letter. Nevertheless, neither expression meant that the writer would necessarily die for you--or even that he intended to pay his bill.

A Mexican would make an appointment with you, but if he decided not to go, he never felt that any great explanation was called for. *Siempre no fuí:* "I just didn't go." Profoundly irritating to Americans, who expected some sort of excuse, however thin. Anyway, come to think of it, the American businessman's "In conference" was about on a par with *Siempre no fuí,* with the veracity heavily on the side of the Mexican. Once my next younger brother, Harry, made a date to play tennis with one Raul at the courts in Gómez Palacio. As this entailed a three-mile ride on the streetcar he was understandably annoyed when Raul failed to show up. Asked about it next day, Raul smiled, shrugged and said, "*Siempre no fuí.*" Harry, ordinarily the kindest and most agreeable of men, was roused to action. He bided his time until Raul suggested a hunting trip. They were to meet at 3:00 A.M. Harry did not appear. And when Raul, exasperated in his turn, asked what had happened, Harry smiled, shrugged and said, "*Siempre no fuí.*"

There were other things that confused and irritated us — in fact, despite the length of time we lived down there we never did get used to some of the facets of Mexican mores. The upper-class Mexicans were for the most part charming people. Many had been educated or had traveled abroad; the women sent to Paris for their clothes (and what clothes!), and they all entertained lavishly and beautifully, and the gifts they gave were almost embarrassingly extravagant. And yet sometimes they violated what to us seemed the basic concept of, not just courtesy, but decency. For instance, Fidi invited a young man to visit us for a week or so. The first night his guest preceded him into the bathroom (we had a real one by that time), and when Fidi entered he found his tootbrush all wet. Questioned, the guest admitted airily that he had used it. Fidi looked at him, picked up the toothbrush and strode to the window. "See this," he cried and hurled it out into the night.

Most of the Mexicans, except those whose ancestry was entirely Spanish, had smooth café-au-lait complexions which accorded well with their dark eyes and lustrous dark hair. Yet the women persisted in using large quantities of flour-white powder. This was at a time when American women had progressed only as far as a touch of rice powder, secretly applied, or a chamois. I don't know whether liquid powder had yet been invented, but whatever the señoras and señoritas used gave the same general effect as calsomine. Once when I was about 13, a most self-conscious age, we were invited to San Pedro to attend a very grand ball given by Francisco Madero (father of the Revolution) for the girl to whom he was engaged. As a special feature of the event all the young girls were supposed to march in two by two, and I, although I was younger than most of them, had been included. My partner was Rosita, aged about 16 and already very much a young lady. She was so thoroughly whitened that she looked like a clown, and I almost balked at walking with her. Just as the procession was about to start Rosita's mother came rushing in, and I gave a sigh of relief, thinking that surely she would do away with some of the girl's make-up. But she only grabbed a powder puff, crying anxiously, "Rosita, ponte más polvito." ("Put on a little more powder!")

The only green spot in Torreón was the plaza. Later it acquired a bandstand and concerts were given daily, but when we arrived it was nothing more than some trees and benches. This was the meeting place, the courting place, and, since it was in the middle of town, the business place also. The principal amusement in any small Mexican town was always the town itself, for the people have an inherent colorfulness, an unconscious grace, that makes them a pleasure to see, and they are incorrigibly interested in everything that happens, no matter how trivial. Everyone lived where he could get the full benefit even if it meant being sandwiched between a couple of noisy *cantinas*. On the evening walks with Mama we went to the plaza and walked around like everyone else. There were two well-defined paths — one for the girls, who moved in giggling groups of three or more, and one for the boys, with the traffic moving in opposite directions so that the girls and boys could see and flirt with each other without bringing down the wrath of the endless assortment of chaperones, who sat on the benches and gossiped.

Courtship in Mexico was achieved by overcoming a most formidable array of obstacles, since every man not absolutely senile was thought of (and probably thought so of himself) as being the most aggressive of Don Juans, from whom no female could possibly be safe. No decent Mexican girl *ever* went with a man anywhere alone, and all younger sisters expected as a matter of course to be dragged along as chaperones. Church, naturally, was the ideal place for private meetings, but even there the girls went in pairs. Any visit to a girl's home was invested with so many maiden aunts, sisters, parents, and other interested relatives that only the most determined suitor ever stuck it out. The system was definitely discouraging to a foreigner, especially the Americans, who were accustomed to a certain amount of freedom in their dealings with young ladies. If a man was looked upon favorably by the girl's family, every member — down to the smallest children — came into the *sala* whenever he came to call.

Apropos of this conception of the Mexican man, once, after I was married, I brought back a quantity of Japanese parasols and lanterns from the United States to be used as cotillion favors at a grand ball that was being given. The idea was that the girls should carry the parasols, the lights should be turned out for a minute, and the men would come hunting their partners with the lighted lanterns. It was an idea that had been used in the States with great enthusiasm, but in Mexico . . . Such an uproar about turning off the lights, and the answer was definitely No. Some of the men, it was felt, might commit abuses—such as stealing a kiss—during that moment of darkness.

Another stumbling block to marriage between foreigners and Mexican girls was the custom that the man should pay all the expenses of the wedding, including the trousseau. Since very few of the foreigners were on a financial parity with the wealthier Mexicans, who were horribly extravagant, marriage was almost an impossibility.

The British and Americans were forced to compromise on certain matters, and it was considered permissible for us to have dates in the afternoon, but not to go unchaperoned at night. (I was secretly engaged for a year, but I never went

WILLIAM JAMIESON, *age 31, about the time of his marriage to Tulitas Wulff in Torreón*

TULITAS (*Dalla*) WULFF *at the age of 19 just before she met her husband*

A Torreón taxi in 1905. These wooden coches with leather curtains were usually dilapidated affairs patronized by the public.

Chalet Wulff, Torreón. Papa's engineering office sits at the foot of the hill.

out alone with Billee in the evening, Papa reluctantly taking me to all the dances). I don't know what the Mexicans thought of this or whether any of my Mexican suitors considered me a light woman — certainly none of them ever offered to "commit any abuses." One of them was a very rich young man from a fine family, who was not only homely but a terrible bore. As a suitor he was indefatigable, coming to call (always with a huge bunch of gardenias) and staying and droning on for hours until I was reduced to calling in first Mama and then Papa to help entertain the man. While Papa talked to him Mama and I would excuse ourselves and go sit in the patio, laughing hysterically at the realization that all we were doing was encouraging him, because naturally he thought that the presence of Mama and Papa meant that his suit was approved. Once he came in the afternoon and I sent out word that I was not at home. He merely said, "I will wait for the Señorita Wulff," and wait he did until nearly dinner time. I was forced to dress, climb over the corral fence, and come in the front door.

Language was a real barrier. I'm sure the French and Germans had trouble discarding their gutteral R's—the Spaniards stubbornly retained their lisp and were dreadfully hard to understand. A sort of pidgin Spanish was evolved — the Chinese became very adept with it, and so did the Americans, Canadians, and English, who for one reason or another, had more trouble learning the language than some of the other foreigners. Part of this may have been lack of ability with languages — certainly a good deal of it stemmed from just plain stubborness on the part of the less well-educated. (My husband, a Canadian, did not come to Mexico until his late twenties, but he applied himself and soon was able to speak well enough to practice medicine.) The classic story along this line is that of the mine foreman who, exasperated by the casual ways of the Mexican workman, cried angrily, "If you savvy in the noche that you ain't a-goin' to trabajar in the mañana, why the hell don't you digame?"

Here again arises the difference between the peon mentality and the middle-class one. The foreman could certainly understand a fellow getting drunk on Sunday and being too hungover to work on Monday—he'd probably done it himself. And regretted the lost day's pay and the fact that whatever he was saving for would have to wait a little longer as a result. The Mexicans, on the other hand, were apt to turn up missing simply because they had enough to eat for the moment and they just didn't feel like working. During the mesquite-bean harvest, for example, they stayed away in droves, living on the beans as long as there were any. Once when Papa was building a dam with a penalty clause in the contract, he was forced to buy up the entire mesquite-bean crop in order to get the thing finished on time.

I have heard people talk about how the foreigners, particularly the Americans, exploited the Mexicans during the era of Porfirio Díaz. Certainly the money for the larger projects stemmed from Wall Street or Threadneedle Street and very probably returned there with a great deal of interest. But the foreigners certainly opened up a lot of new jobs, and brought to Mexico new methods, new ideas, new ways of handling matters which gave the country a big shove toward the twentieth century. The foreigners who came in to offer services, to open stores, laundries, to be bookkeepers, doctors, lawyers, and so on, were risking their own capital and their own futures, and they involved themselves heavily in whatever they were doing. So, too, the managers of mines and cotton plantations, ranches and other such. In this way they gave Mexico a glimpse of middle-class thinking which came in very handy during the Revolution when the old status was finally overthrown. In the long run, I'm inclined to think that Mexico, whether she believes it or not, owes a great deal to those foreigners.

Chapter VI — SERVANTS

W A WHOLE BOOK could be written about Mexican servants of that period. Now, doubtless, they are better educated, less superstitious, economically better off, I hope, and possibly less willing and pleasant to have around. At any rate, when I lived down there they were definitely part of the picture, and the one absolute necessity, aside from food and shelter, was the *mozo*. The nearest English equivalent is handyman, but the *mozo* covered a lot more territory and he was constantly on the run.

Our front door on that first house was enormous — it would have come in handy in a medieval fortress — and it was locked with a key a foot long and correspondingly heavy. Since it was impossible for any of us to carry it around, our *mozo* always slept, wrapped in a *sarape* with only his nose showing, on the floor of the *zaguán* to admit the late comers. At 4:30 in the morning he arose, tied a dirty handkerchief over his nose and went out to sweep the sidewalk. All the other *mozos* were doing the same thing, and as the walk was made of brick which had been insufficiently fired, the whole neighborhood suffered a tornado of brick dust despite all the buckets of water they sloshed around.

After that he milked the cows, fed the chickens, gathered the eggs, scrubbed the floors, brought in wood for the stoves, emptied ashes, and went on countless errands. He went for the doctor, delivered messages, social and otherwise, all over town, went for the ice and to the market a half dozen times a day for forgotten items. Later on when telephones did arrive in Torreón they did nothing to ease the *mozo's* burden. For instead of one phone system they put in two, and you could talk only to people who had the same system you did. Of course, you could be extravagant and have both, but the service was uniformly awful, and on the whole it was easier to send the *mozo*, just as we always had.

Nothing was ever on time down there. Theatrical performances began whenever enough audience had accumulated and the players felt the urge to begin emoting, so the *mozo* always had to make several trips to case the situation and tell us when it was time to go. The theater was simply an open-air affair with a platform at one end, a fence defining the area, and, inexplicably, an old well boarded over in the middle. There was no nonsense about reservations or advance ticket sales. People took their own chairs to the theater and set them wherever they thought they would have the best view — if you owned no chairs, you sat on the ground. This meant the *mozo* had to take our chairs over earlier. If by any chance it began to rain, he ran back to the house for umbrellas or newspapers — entertainment was too scarce to pass up for anything less than a deluge. If one of us had fallen into the well, he would no doubt have had to fish us out. But he didn't mind this aspect of his work too much, since he got to sit on the ground and enjoy the performance too.

Social engagements were equally uncertain, and we always sent the *mozo* several times before we dared start anywhere, because dinners set for eight seldom began before ten, and if we had arrived on time, our hosts probably would not have been dressed.

Train service was just as dilatory. The engineers considered themselves very important men — if one had a girl he wanted to visit, the train could wait till he did so. So the *mozo* always made several trips to the station and when premonitory rumblings and shiftings indicated that the schedule was about to go into operation again he rushed home to inform us, summon a *coche,* and load the bags into it.

There were a million other jobs for the *mozo,* including saddling and otherwise taking care of the two ponies and the other horses we acquired from time to time. When Papa grew affluent enough to build the big house on the hill he built a swimming pool too, and the *mozo* took care of that. Oh, well, he did whatever had to be done, and for all this he was paid the munificent sum of 10 pesos a month (about $5 then). When out of ignorance and generosity Papa started our first *mozo* at 12 pesos he was bitterly criticized for spoiling the labor market. (It was not entirely ignorance, at that, for the man was unusually capable.) On this amount, that first *mozo* managed to support a wife and five children besides contributing heavily to the local *cantinas.* He was with us a number of years and, despite the drinking, was a faithful, loyal and conscientious employee. In fact, as I look back on the many servants we had throughout those years I realize that the majority were faithful and conscientious. But, as in any other concentration of people, there were exceptions. Some of our *mozos* showed remarkable ingenuity and enterprise.

José, for instance, used the early morning hours, while he swept the sidewalk, to sell our eggs to a select clientele of his own. We had sixty chickens and never got an egg. When questioned he always insisted that the hens laid their eggs under the wood pile where he couldn't reach them. When the woodpile was, presumably, one vast omelet, someone got up early enough to catch him, and another small business-man was out of business. At least with our eggs.

Alberto, whom we suspected of being a trifle light-fingered, was sent to the market one day to make some last-minute purchase. On the way he passed a small carnival, was tempted and fell. He used the money to buy a ticket on the ferris wheel. Never was retribution swifter or more fitting — Gilbert and Sullivan would have been in ecstasies. For when he reached the top of the wheel the machinery broke and he had to stay up there all night. We never saw Alberto again — he was, we heard, too ashamed.

The train tracks, as I have mentioned, ran right through town and trains were often parked for hours, so that you had to make a wide detour around them. If you were afoot and daring enough, sometimes you took a chance and crawled over the couplings between the cars. Epimeño, another *mozo*, was sent to get a fifty-pound cake of ice. Returning, the ice firmly tied with a piece of rope, he found his way barred by a long freight which had just pulled in and seemed likely to stay awhile. Epimeño decided to chance it, but just as he was crawling through, the train started off and he was carried to Gómez Palacio, three miles away, before he could dismount. Having no money for the streetcar, he walked home in the blazing sun. The ice was long since melted when he got back, but he proudly showed us that the rope was still wet, evidence that he had really bought the ice.

Atilano was one of our best *mozos,* and he was so talented at painting, papering, plastering and carpentry that he finally went into business for himself. He was very tall and had very thick straight hair, which was never combed or washed. When we met him on the street there was no need to ask what he had been doing—the hair told it all, like a gourmand's vest. There was the green paint from Mrs. So-and-so's newly re-done *sala*, the plaster from the new *cantina,* sawdust from the addition to the brewery and so on. Incidentally, during the Revolution Atilano had his chance. He came up in the world, became one of the new middle class, made money. When Papa met him on the street one day he hardly recognized the man — he wore a regular business suit, a shirt and tie, and his hair had been cut and shone with brilliantine.

It was at this time also (during the Revolution) that Papa, anticipating that Villa would besiege Torreón, had the swimming pool, which was in a little house of its own, thoroughly scrubbed and disinfected and filled with drinking water, just in case. Then he locked the place up. One day, though, passing by, he heard a strange noise and discovered that one of our old *mozos*, having retained a key to the place, was having himself a fine swim.

If the *mozo* did the marketing, he was usually willing to come for a little less, haggling joyously over every purchase and picking up a few *centavos* for himself in the process. This applied to the cook also, the next most important member of the hierarchy. Old María, who cooked for me after I was married, used to sit on the sidewalk and compute her "take" with *frijoles*, since she could neither read nor write.

This bargaining, as in many other countries, was an intrinsic part of the shopping and most of the fun. (It is not a part of the culture of the United States, which may be why we do so poorly in international give and take.) One American, against all advice, set up a one-price store in Torreón and speedily went broke, although his wares were better and cheaper. But it just wasn't any fun shopping there. After all, if you have only a *centavo* or two to spend, it's lots less interesting to just walk in and pay the price.

Another interesting facet of the customs was that Saturday was begging day, and many of the servants reserved the right to go begging on that day. The storekeepers set aside one portion of their counters on which they put a number of *centavos*, and each beggar entered, took only one coin, and left for the next shop. I don't know whether this custom still obtains in Mexico, but it's the only thing that explains what I read in the paper several years ago, that the beggars union in Mexico City had gone on strike for higher alms.

At the time we lived in Torreón, the cooks seldom cooked anything except Mexican foods and some simpler foreign dishes. The fancy German and French cookery was for the most part quite beyond them except under the closest supervision. This seems odd, for many Mexican dishes take as much time and effort as any other culinary masterpiece. *Mole*, for example, can have as many as fifty ingredients. Incidentally, the cook (or *mozo*) was usually given extra money to buy food for herself and the other servants. They did not eat what we ate except for Mexican food, as buying foreign food for them would have been too expensive and not tempting to them anyway. Groceries were kept locked up and doled out every day.

Frequently you hired a whole family — the mother cooked, the daughters cleaned and washed, the son or father was the *mozo*. One such family, eight in all, worked for Mrs. Carothers, wife of the American Consul in Torreón, for many years. When the Revolution got hotter and diplomatic relations between the two countries more strained, Mrs. Carothers, knowing that she would be leaving soon, called the servants in and explained carefully that she intended to withhold part of their wages every payday, so that when she was gone they would have a nice little nest egg to tide them over. They all nodded and agreed to the arrangement, but as time passed they became surly and troublesome. So Mrs. C. called in old Juana, the cook and mother, and asked what the trouble was.

"Señora, how can you expect us to do good work when you are not paying us our full wages?" Juana asked in return.

Mrs. Carothers went over the whole thing again, but Juana merely repeated obdurately that they couldn't be happy working at such wages, and her mistress gave up, pulled out the accumulated savings and turned it over. They promptly decided to have a *fiesta*, which not only included food and drink for all their friends and relatives but eighty *pesos* for an eight-foot *santo* (image of a saint) to grace the occasion — and blew the whole amount in one night.

In families where there were children there was usually a nursemaid for each small child. These were called *nanas*, and there was great rivalry and sometimes jealousy between them over the merits and charms of their individual charges.

Servants came and went, often quitting for no apparent reason. Usually they told some long improbable story about a dying relative in Guanajuato or some place equally distant who could not be able to rest comfortably in his coffin without at least a glimpse of the Torreón cousin. This was because the peculiar *Americanos* always insisted on knowing why they were leaving. Otherwise they simply vanished, and we would see them later working at someone else's house. Also, they were usually very superstitious, and if one decided his employer had a *mal de ojo* (evil eye) he would take off. (Sometimes he would communicate his convictions about the quality of his ex-employer's gaze, and it would be very difficult for that family to get any servants at all.)

Later on, after I was married, I had a mother and daughter working for me, Sara and Manuela. Manuela was totally deaf but a good worker when her mother could communicate sufficiently with her. When Sara wanted Manuela to come upstairs, she simply threw the broom down the stairs. One day when I was giving a dinner party Sara received a message from someone, and she came rushing in to tell me that she and Manuela would have to leave immediately. I was irritated because the day before had been a special saint's day and they had had the afternoon off. I expostulated, Sara insisted it was a matter of life and death, and I demanded details.

"Well," she explained, "my father-in-law is very very sick, and nothing will cure him except a hair from the tail of a black cat. Manuela and I have to go get that hair."

Generally when the servants quit there was no great problem, however. All you had to do was go outside and hail the first possible-looking idler. Usually he (or she) "didn't care if" he did work awhile.

Once just before a dinner party the *mozo* took French leave, so Papa went out into the street to find a substitute — we needed a waiter. He was lucky enough to find a man dressed in a fairly respectable frock coat, with a mustache and imperial, obviously fresh from the barber's chair. All afternoon long we trained Tomás in what he was to do, and he was a very apt pupil — one might have almost said he had a flair for it. When he took off the frock coat he'd had on all afternoon his shirt turned out to be clean and not too shabby. Mama handed him one of the long aprons waiters wore in those days and went out to greet her guests, happily conscious that things were going well. Presently Tomás entered the *sala*, bearing a tray of aperitifs and doing a most professional job. Then he turned to leave and there was a concerted gasp from the guests. He had no seat in his trousers!

Chapter VII

THE WULFFS AND THE GROOSES

ᴗ PAPA WAS BORN in San Antonio on January 4, 1856. His father, Anton Frederick Wulff, came to Texas from Hamburg, Germany, in 1848, settling first in New Braunfels, that mecca of German immigrants. He moved to San Antonio later and in 1852 married María Guadalupe Olivarri, a descendant of one of the Canary Island families who were sent to settle in Texas around 1720 by the King of Spain. The king sent with them complete instructions for every detail of their lives, including the number of homes to be built, number of rooms for each home, and everything else. They settled what was called San Fernando, and either because they were just naturally snooty or because they had had such personal attention from the king, other colonists found them stiffnecked and hard to get along with. But by the time the Germans arrived they had evidently mellowed enough to intermarry with the newcomers.

Much later Anton, at the instigation of his children, wrote an account of his early life:

> At the age of 22 years on the 13th of May, 1843, I left my homeland, Hamburg, and arrived in Paris on the 22nd of May, 1843. I traveled as a drummer to Belgium, Holland and Germany and was in Hamburg shortly after the Great Fire. I left Paris in April 1848, after Louis Philipp fled to England. I saw the plundering of the Tuilleries and the barricades in Paris. On Friday morning, the 17th of June, 1848, I left Ham-

burg on the sailing ship, *Pentucket* (Capt. Taylor). After a 65-day trip I saw the outline of New York on August 22.

From New York I traveled on without a plan, as I was not able to secure employment there or in Cincinnati. I then traveled down the Mississippi to New Orleans. There my funds gave out and I made the acquaintance of a theologian named Schmidt whose destination was Texas, which in those days was considered a discredited land and was described as such even in New Orleans. I disregarded these reports and accepted the offer of my new friend to go to New Braunfels, Texas, to establish a grocery business there. We left New Orleans by schooner and landed with our wares in Lavaca, Texas, after a 6-day trip. Our first dinner on our trip by stage was in Victoria where they gave us many good things; pumpkins, sweet potatoes, bacon and molasses. Though it didn't look very good, it was pretty enjoyable for us.

We arrived at last in New Braunfels. My first ride was to San Marcos to find the guides who had been delayed a long time. On arrival in Seguin, I, who had never been on a horse, was so stiff that I could barely get out of the saddle. I wanted to stay in San Marcos overnight, but I lost my way and arrived at night in Seguin, where a strapping American woman, with a pipe in her mouth, greeted me and took me in. Corn, bacon and coffee was our evening meal. My bed for the night was large enough for three, but I found in the morning they had put in another man. As I had found my guides the night before camped in San Marcos, I was able to start my trip back.

My theologian friend didn't much relish the idea of the grocery store, so he bought a farm on the Cibolo and I was to help farm.

Our start as farmers was not very encouraging after the oxen, with the plow borrowed from a neighbor named Jones, ran 1½ miles away. I found my shoes full of dirt and I decided that I was not fitted for farming. I was then able, after having been in San Antonio, to procure a position as clerk, from 6 a.m. to 9 or 10 at night, for $5 a month. Worth mentioning are persons I met during visits where we drank whiskey: Dr. Koerner, Graf Hendel von Donnersmark who married his cook; Baron von Schuetze; Lawyer Fisher; Father Confessor Paul, and others. My entrance into San Antonio at night in the dark was not very notable in that the mule I rode went off at a gallop and threw me off on the corner of Main Plaza, so I had to continue on foot. The next day I found my mule well cared for in a livery stable.

My investment of $5 for my share in the farm was lost. After James R. Sweet, father of the Texas Siftings, also entered as clerk, we both worked as clerks and porters. I was able to better my position by entering the employ of Landa, who had a little store on the corner where Frost's Bank now is. The salary was $30 on which I was able to save, so that James R. Sweet, who had established his own business, made me an offer to go to Fredericksburg and open a business for him with a share in it. With my savings I was able to buy a good horse, gun and pistol, so I rode there alone.

My business was soon established and doing well, so I decided to look for a wife, after I had declared my intentions of becoming an American citizen (in 1852) and received my papers in Fredericksburg. Though the life at that time was lonely, there were diversions such as the trade with the Indians. These were Lipans, Mescaleros, Comanches, Cados, Kickapoos, Cobos and Delawares. The Delawares often acted as guides to the American troops then stationed at Fort Martin Scott. William Kook was my first employee and cook and later Herr Weis, uncle of Golfrank, my clerk.

After I bought a house in Fredericksburg and built an addition in the neighborhood of the Lutheran Church called the Coffee Mill, I went in search of a life partner, in which Tio Julio, a well known personality in San Antonio, was very helpful. I saw your mother for the first time at a little dance on Commerce Street, where Mr. Groos now lives, and there we became acquainted. On Nov. 20, 1852, we were married in the house of John James in the presence of Josefa Rodriguez and a sister of your mother's. After a few years and I had earned $5,000, Sweet made me an offer to take over his business with Bart J. DeWitt, to which I agreed and sold out to Wahrmund. The business did not do so well although it was on Main Street. During that time I built the house which is still standing on the east side of the river. We gave up our business since I still had a business on Oak Creek on the Concho which Leindecker at that time was running. I gave that up too. We met many Indians, who were friendly, except the Lipans and Comanches who were enemies. Later I made an inspection trip to Laredo, where we had a side business for a time.

The firm of S. Mayer and Coda, the well known wholesale and retail dry goods firm which conducted considerable business in Chihuahua, Mex., inspired me to go to Presidio Del Norte, at that time the place second in importance to Chihuahua.

After I had already made an inspection trip by horseback to Laredo, which at that time made an undesirable impression on me, I decided to go to Presidio Del Norte. In order to do this, I gave Mayer & Co. my order to sell my house for $5,000. Mayer himself bought it and later lived in it for a long time.

We made the trip with *carreten* (wagons) partly owned by Tio Trinidad. There were 9 of us who went along: Mama, Heinrich with Fritz and Leonides went in an ambulance while Mariano and Inez and Pablo (the latter a Caudillo or boy stolen by the Indians whom I had bought from them in Fredericksburg) and a boat which we took along on a *carreta*. From San Antonio I took 2 clerks, one a Mr. Hagelsieb and a Mexican. The trip took us 7 weeks. After we had installed ourselves and had opened the business, I took an inspection trip to Mexico, direct to Santa Rosalía. There I later opened a second business for a short time.

The day of our arrival in Santa Rosalía I met a troop of the friendlier Indians just in sight of town. They had come the same way we had the day before. They had killed and wounded several Mexicans, stolen their horses and gone on their way.

From Santa Rosalía I took a side trip to the mining town of Parral. When I returned, Fritz had the smallpox. We cured him without a doctor and the disease was mild and left no scars. I had seen enough of Mexico after 8 months and went to Presidio and established a business on the Mexican side where we stayed until the outbreak of the Civil War. My trips often took me to Chihuahua where I made purchases. At that time there were quite a number of Germans like the Moye brothers, Carlos Gustav and Wilhelm and Emil Schetelig, and others. In San Pablo there was Guillermo Talamantes. In those days they were nearly all wealthy; now all are dead but Emil. The Mexicans were friendly people like Feliz Mayra, Juan Terrazas, the governor, and friendly Frenchmen such as Victor Yrigoite and Pedro Mignagoren.

On one of my last trips there in September, 1860, it happened that the River Conchos, which I had to cross, was very high, and I probably would have had to wait 8 days before I could cross. I had an ambulance with about $4,000, silk dresses for Mama, and a few Chihuahua dogs, and therefore did not want to wait. As the river was about half a mile wide, a friend, the Alcalde Julian Muñoz, suggested I make a raft. We went to work right away. We took the wheels off the wagon, and then the mules and my horse were led on by 2 Mexicans. Our trip started with my friend Muñoz and 10 Mexicans as swimmers. I undressed and my *mozo*, Eustaquio, led the ferry. It was immediately apparent that the wood of the raft was green as it sank almost at once about 8 inches under the water. The stream took us along. Often we passed tree trunks and were always in danger of tipping over, but that was the reason for the swimmers. It was very cold and they were in the water shivering for 5 hours, but we made it and landed on a sandbank.

From there I and all the rest were carried over to the bank and we spent the night there. This was by Julienes, where a large crowd came running to us, as the report had been that we had all been drowned. With all this, nothing was lost, and I saw that not everyone steals. Eustaquio, a wonderful swimmer, had carried a large knife between his teeth the whole time, and he explained later that it was to cut the raft apart in case it looked as though we might drown, so that we might save ourselves. The following day we continued our journey, and after 1½ days were back in Presidio. There was great rejoicing at our arrival, since they had heard that we had all drowned.

As I rode to Ft. Davis, where I had large contracts for hay and corn, we heard that the Secession War had been declared and, as the troops were to march to San Antonio, the business came to an end.

Shortly after the Confederate troops were seen and came over to the Mexican side, and they came into my store. They said they wanted to buy horses and tried to persuade me to come over to the Texas side. I would not agree to this as I did not want to have anything to do with them.

This was the end of Anton's story and he obviously left out a great deal. The story in the family is that the Confederate troops, finding him obdurate, then tried to kidnap him, and that the citizens, roused by his brother-in-law, came to the rescue.

The Civil War proved a source of great embarrassment to the Germans in Texas and probably to other foreigners. They were not slaveholders, despite Anton's mention of the boy he bought from the Indians, and few had any ties with the deep South. Their sympathies, if any, would probably have been with the North, but that was a long way away, and they preferred just to sit the war out. Anton actually took his family to Germany, back to Hamburg, for the duration, and Granpa Groos moved to Mexico, where the French depleted him with forced loans.

When he returned to the United States, Anton ran wagon trains from Chihuahua, where he subsequently established a store, to San Antonio, carrying goods one way and loose wheat the other. Under the wheat were pine boxes packed with silver pesos, the fruit of all these transactions. The money was taken to his house and stored under guard, as there were no banks. Papa, as a small boy, went along on the wagon trains and used to tell about one trip when they were attacked by Indians. The reference to Fritz (that is, Papa) having had the smallpox omits the interesting information that Heinrich (Uncle Henry) got it first and they made Papa sleep with him so he would get it and get it over with.

Anton also omits the information that he was mad about flowers and gardens, and that he gave several pieces of property to the town of San Antonio for parks. They promptly made him the first park commissioner, a job he fulfilled with interest and talent.

Granpa Groos, like Anton, had been educated in Germany and found his degree in architecture and civil engineering of little use in the wilderness of Texas. He and his brothers also went into merchandising, and later on they did a little banking on the side purely as an accommodation. The banking soon became more important than the rest of the business, and in 1897 they built a handsome new building, the first exclusively for the use of the bank.

Mama's name was Linda and she was plump, dark and gay, and very pretty. She loved going places and doing things, and I am sure that the very limited social and cultural opportunities in Torreón must have been a disappointment to her. But she also possessed the wonderful gift of enjoying even the smallest thing. She wasn't much of a housekeeper but she was a marvelous hostess, and she certainly had plenty of chances to exercise her talents along that line. Both Papa and Mama were incurably hospitable, and there were always guests at our house, family, friends, even friends of friends. Some of them stayed long enough to go into business in Torreón.

One of the more frequent visitors was Mama's oldest sister, Carlota, whom we called Tante Lotts. She was tall and thin with long narrow hands and feet, and she looked almost exactly like her father, which was unfortunate. He was a handsome man in a craggy way, and his features did not translate well into a feminine mold, especially in the period when women were supposed to be pale, delicate flowers.

Granpa Groos was an austere man, who saw to it that his children had good serviceable clothes, plenty of good food, and the best education the period afforded. But no frivolity or foolishness. In Mama's childhood, when hoopskirts were fashionable, she and her sisters were not allowed to wear their hoops to school — they had to be saved for Sundays.

Tante Lotts wanted to be a farmer, but that was unthinkable for a well-brought-up young lady then, so I doubt seriously that she ever mentioned the matter to her father. I don't know whether she ever had any beaux or even wanted any — at any rate she never married. By modern standards she was probably frustrated as anyone you could find and undoubtedly should have "gone on the tiles" or taken up burglary. But she didn't — she devoted her life to mothering people — her youngest sister, Carrie, and a flock of nieces and nephews, of whom we were the most numerous and most impecunious.

Perhaps because of this frustration Tante Lotts was troubled all her life by a vast indecisiveness. Although they were wealthy, the girls seldom saw any cash money. Once, however, Granpa Gross came home with some newly minted 50¢ pieces, which he gave to the children. They rushed off to squander this fabulous sum, and Mama, always quick and sure, found something she liked immediately. So did the others — except Carlota. Finally Mama said, "Well, if you can't make up your mind, give me the money. I see something else I want."

Carlota, exhausted by her dilemma, was only too glad to comply, but their father, on hearing the story, was furious. He sent them back to the store with instructions to return the article bought and then, if Carlota still couldn't decide, Mama was to buy something for her. She did — a pair of sleeve garters.

Carlota's inability to make up her mind was just as agonizing to the clerks in stores when she was grown up. I'm sure they must have dreaded her appearance, although she was the soul of courtesy and a very good customer indeed. I went shopping with her once, and the procedure ran something like this. First she put her outsize purse, roughly the size of a small suitcase, on the counter. Then she took out one of her other two pair of glasses. This was a major operation involving much scavenging in the bottom of the bag, where keys, handkerchiefs, two change purses (one for the nickels, dimes and pennies, the other for quarters and half dollars), another purse for the bills (the dirty things carefully wrapped in tissue paper), and several other items lurked. Then she would start looking at the merchandise, an interminable operation which once almost got her arrested for shoplifting. She suffered greatly from the heat and except in the dead of winter always carried a fan in her purse. Once, while trying to buy a new fan, she tucked one she rather liked under one arm, another she considered possible under the other arm. Then she finally did decide on still another one, she paid for it and started out of the store with the first two, quite forgotten, still under her arms. The clerk caught her just as she reached the street. Poor Tante Lotts probably died a thousand deaths over the whole unfortunate episode.

Once when I was visiting in San Antonio she asked me to help her decide which hose would match her dress best. Since she wore ankle-length dresses and Ground Gripper oxfords, the question did not seem very pressing, but, naturally, I said I'd be glad to. She produced thirteen pairs of service-weight stockings, each a slightly different shade of beige!

She saved string till she had a ball the size of a beach ball, saved a closet full of wrapping paper and paper sacks, and boxes until she had a pile that reached almost to the twelve-foot ceiling. She saved crumbs for the birds, although I never heard of any birds dying of starvation in San Antonio's mild climate. She insisted that the yard man take wheelbarrow loads of grass cuttings to a neighbor who owned a cow. She contributed to charities and civic causes, helped out nieces and nephews when they were in tight spots. And all her life, although she lived to be over eighty, she always went up the stairs on the inside, where the steps narrowed to nothingness, in order, she said, that the staircase "might wear out evenly."

Chapter VIII — PAPA

Ꙩ IN 1871 PAPA, his next two brothers, Triny and Henry, and Mama's two brothers, Fritz and Charlie, were sent to school in Germany. The trip was complicated. They went by stage to Columbus, then the nearest railroad station to San Antonio. (This may mean Columbus, Louisiana — I am not sure.) From there by train to Lake Pontchartrain where they boarded a steamer and went up along the East Coast to New York. From New York by Hamburg-American liner to Germany, a twelve-day trip. In Hamburg they saw the victorious Prussian troops returning from France after the Franco-Prussian War.

They were supposed to enter the Politecnicum, a preparatory school, but they were too young and had to spend one year in a private school. Papa did not say whether they had any vacations and if so, what they did or where they spent them — certainly they must have had relatives in Germany. Papa then took the examinations for the Politecnicum and spent a year there. After more exams he was finally admitted to the University of Hanover for the four-year course in civil engineering and architecture. The class initially consisted of 100 young men — at the end of the four years Papa was one of four survivors.

The other boys did not stay so long. Granpa Wulff fell and broke a leg, leaving him crippled for life, and Henry was called home to help with the business. Why the others didn't stay on I have no idea.

Papa alone remained in Germany, and while he must have suffered some homesickness, I suppose, on the whole he enjoyed himself hugely. The University of Hanover, being a scientific school, had no dueling customs, but the students, nevertheless, had to have plenty of stamina. There were many drinking clubs, and each one had its distinctive headgear. Each club had some forty or fifty members, and each new initiate was required to "bottoms up" a stein of beer with every other member individually!

Nowadays there is a good deal of talk and writing about letting your subconcious work for you, and there are records, particularly foreign-language ones, which are supposed to din knowledge into your head while you sleep. Perhaps the principle involved is guiding the brain in the way it should go instead of letting it wander around in the absurdities of dreams, and it does seem too bad not to let the poor thing have some rest and relaxation. (I won't go into more recent discoveries which seem to indicate that dreaming keeps the brain from giving up in sheer despair or something.) Anyway, nearly all of us have dreamed of solving some pressing problem — some authors dream up the most wonderful plots. Once when Papa was a senior the class was given a very long and difficult engineering problem to solve. They were given three weeks to do it, and they spent every minute on the thing without getting very far. As the deadline neared Papa's subconscious took on the job and he dreamed the solution. He awoke, still full of the dream, and rushed over to the desk and wrote it down. Then he went back to bed. When he woke in the morning he wasn't sure that he hadn't dreamed the whole business, but sure enough, the pen and inkpot were out on the desk. He arose, trembling with excitement, and ran to the desk. There was the paper and on it a lot of scratches, like hen tracks!

Some of his vacations he spent wandering up and down the Rhine, enjoying the food, the people, the magnificent scenery. One summer he decided he would like to spend the time working, and having read about the new launching method which they were inaugurating at the Royal Navy Yard at Kiel, thought he would like to work there. But when he mentioned it, his classmates hooted. The German Court was formal to the point of stuffiness — why, they said, it would take a lawyer just to write the letter asking to be allowed to go there. But being an American, Papa was not impressed. He wrote a letter to Gentlemen, asking to be allowed to work for nothing during the summer, signed F. Wulff. Maybe it was this piece of effrontery that intrigued them or, more likely, curiosity about him as an American — there had been very few Americans in Germany up to that time. In any event, he was invited to spend the summer working there, and, moreover, they offered to pay him for his services.

The chief engineer at the Navy Yard was greatly taken with Papa and his stories about the United States, particularly the Indians. The Indians around San Antonio at that time were pretty tame, but this was the period when the Apaches, Comanches and Sioux were kicking up their heels in the West.

Of course, the big thing at the Navy Yard was the launching to come. The channel was very narrow, so that a ship sliding down the ways had to be swung about sharply. A tremendous chain had been devised, with links a yard long and proportionately wide, and the weight of this was supposed to swing the ship around into the channel. The ship to be launched was the first armored one, and although the Emperor was not coming, Admiral Von Stosch and a lot of top brass were expected.

When the chief engineer showed Papa the chain and asked his opinion, Papa remarked that the ship would not go one-third of the distance across the channel so the thing was unnecessary.

"How do you know?" Schmidt demanded, startled at what amounted to *lese majeste*.

"I just feel it," said Papa.

"In Wilhelmshafen," Schmidt replied stiffly, "we do not feel. We calculate."

But when the ship was launched with much fanfare, it happened just as Papa had predicted. Schmidt then took Papa into his office, sent out all the other employees, and asked, "How did you know? How did you find the error in the calculations?"

"I just felt it," Papa repeated.

"Oh, come now, how can a layman feel better than we can calculate?"

"Well, when you throw a stone, can't you feel about where it will go?" Papa countered.

With some surprise Schmidt agreed that this was so, and thereafter he called Papa the man with the practical feeling.

His schoolmates had long since christened him the Practical American, because he possessed, like most Americans, a certain mechanical knack which the Germans seemed to lack. However, maybe this is partly environmental because Papa said that when he got home he felt clumsy and awkward with tools alongside his brothers.

Papa was very musical, and one of the things he enjoyed most about his school years was the marvelous opportunity for hearing good music, particularly in Germany, which was in the throes of a great musical period. The orchestra considered the best in the country was in Hanover, directed by Von Bülow. Later it went to the Metropolitan in New York. Papa traveled to Vienna to hear Johann Strauss. And in Hanover he heard Wagner himself conduct *Tannhauser*. The students were so excited that they picked Wagner up and carried him on their shoulders to his hotel. Bellini conducted the *Barber of Seville* there, and Rubinstein, Clara Schumann and Sarasate all came there at one time or another. One concert was given by Liszt, who was then at the Abbey, to present his star pupil. They played piano duets with Liszt sitting behind a screen. The ovation was so tremendous that Liszt was moved to come out from behind the screen and play two of Brahms' *Hungarian Waltzes*. It was the music Papa missed most when he finally graduated and came home.

Chapter IX — MEXICAN MEDICINE

W PASTEUR'S GERM THEORY was still relatively new when we went to live in Mexico, and hygiene was not a burning issue anywhere. In Mexico it was unheard of. Although we had medicines of various kinds, the only sort of antiseptic we had was vinegar — not that we knew anything about antisepsis, but that was standard treatment for a cut. I don't recall that anything was done to the well water after the chicken was fished out. All the windows in the house were barred except the one in the kitchen, but there were no screens, and there were plenty of flies, mosquitoes in season, roaches and other vermin. The chickens hopped in and out of the kitchen with cozy informality, picking up crumbs off the floor and sometimes flying up to the table to join the servants in their meal. Sometimes the corral gate would be left open and larger stock would wander in. The house had no closets, just big old-fashioned wardrobes, and since furniture was expensive and hard to get, we had to resort to various odd expedients to accommodate the endless round of guests. Once when Udo, a cousin, was there Mama gave him a bookcase to keep his clothes in — or on. Every morning one of the hens would wander in, deposit an egg on his underwear, cackle cheerily to wake him up, and then depart. Udo bore up under this nicely, being at an age when underwear was not important, but he did object when the calf strolled in and licked his face.

The Saturday-night bath was customary, and we objected as small children usually do. One of our complaints was that we had just a plain old bathtub, whereas the Severins had a

German one. This was a fascinating object. It was set on rockers and at one end the tin of which it was made came up over the top, rather like a baby buggy top. When you sat in the tub and rocked, the water would go into this top and come down over you like a shower. We were all dying to take a bath in that tub, but since there were almost as many Severins as there were Wulffs, we were never invited.

I'm sure we caught most of the childhood diseases, and naturally when one of us caught something we had our own private epidemic, but we were spared diphtheria, scarlet fever and smallpox. I think we must have been vaccinated before we went down to Mexico, for smallpox was so prevalent there that it ranked with chickenpox and mumps. So many generations had had the disease that many of the cases were very light, although there were plenty of deaths too. The Mexicans took it very calmly. One doctor, examining a child, asked what diseases it had had.

"Nothing," replied the mother, "not even the smallpox."

The Mexicans had their own cures, mostly herb teas which they brewed and which probably had some merit, like other folk medicine. They also had some rather horrifying practices such as, for example, hanging a woman in the throes of a difficult birth up over a fire. One very potent remedy was a sort of paste made out of tomatoes, supposed to be especially efficacious for chickens with roup. A friend of ours suffered greatly from asthma, and there was only one doctor in town who seemed to be able to help her much. Once when he was out of town she got sick, and her cook said, "Señora, if you won't let me call another doctor, at least try one of my remedies." By this time the woman would have tried almost anything, so the cook smeared her throat with the tomato paste and then tied three *tortillas* around it. There is evidence now that asthma is at least partly psychological. Anyway, medicinal or psychological, it worked.

Dysentery, like the poor, was always with us, but we acquired a certain imperviousness after awhile. Not that we were immune, but that it seldom happened and was usually not too serious. Once when Papa was building a dam out in the wilderness, miles from anywhere, he did get a bad dose of it. One of his laborers offered him a cure — flour and water mixed to a thick paste. Papa finally managed to down this horrible concoction and it worked.

In Zaragosa, a tiny town not many miles from Torreón, there was an outbreak of diphtheria, and a Canadian doctor from a nearby hacienda was called in. He immediately said that the only thing that would prevent a really serious epidemic was a strict quarantine, adding, "But, of course, you'd never do that."

The *jefe* replied, "Why, certainly we will. We'll station a soldier in front of the door of every house where there is a case of diphtheria, and he'll see to it that no one enters except the most important people."

A German family in Torreón lost their oldest girl to scarlet fever when she was about eight years old. When the second girl reached the same age she also developed the disease and died, and the same thing happened to the third girl. The doctors later decided that the coat and hat which the first child had worn when she got sick and which had been thriftily put away and then used again when the other two girls were the right size had apparently retained the germs and infected each in turn.

The Mexicans did not believe in bathing very often, although the women were always shampooing their hair and going around with it hanging like a damp curtain over a bath towel pinned on their backs. It was considered very dangerous to bathe in winter and possibly in those little icy huts (there is nothing colder than a Mexican *jacal*) they were right. Others carried it further, confining their ablutions to the 24th of June, San Juan's day. I don't know why unless he was the patron saint of soap. They all wore the Mexican *huaraches,* and the leather was tanned somehow to make it peculiarly odoriferous. When combined with feet washed only on the 24th of June, the results were almost unbearable. Once when Bub and Chulo, the two youngest children, were playing in the doorway, as children always seem to do, the *mozo* kept going back and forth with loads of wood for the stoves.

"Here he comes again, Bub," Chulo was heard to say as the man approached. "Hold your breathing."

As a matter of convenience the outhouse had to be cleaned out periodically, and this was done for us by a man with a horse and wagon. Appropriately enough, he was named Narciso, and he charged so much a barrel. All this was done in the dead of night at a time which those of us who were unlucky enough to wake up had dubbed the Smelly Hour. Usually the *mozo* oversaw the operation, but once Papa, feeling that he was being overcharged, went out to superintend. It was a dark night and he couldn't see, but it seemed to him that the first barrel was filled entirely too rapidly. He asked sharply if the barrel was full. Narciso asserted positively that it was.

"How do you know?" Papa demanded suspiciously.

"Why," Narciso explained simply, "I just stuck my hand in."

I never saw Narciso but I often wondered about him. What would prompt a man to go into a business like that? Probably, I realized, he didn't think about it at all—it was a living, somebody had to do it, and, most important, he was self-employed. Mexicans love that — better a *puesto* (stall) in the market waving a horsetail flywhisk over six oranges than a clerk in a store at twice the money. This fierce independence was always latent, but since few of them were ever in a position to do much about it, it was apt to manifest itself in a touchiness about "honor" which struck foreigners as highly exaggerated.

Not quite duels over doughnuts, but close to it. Charles Flandrau mentions the same thing in his *Viva Mexico* where the boy who did the errands in town had been stealing with regularity a piece of the meat every time the butcher in town had any. They knew about it because his mother had had the nerve to complain to the butcher when the meat was tough. Finally when the boy brought back such a tiny piece of meat that it seemed too obvious to ignore, they accused him of it. There was a big scene — his honor had been impugned, he could no longer work there, and his mother declared fiercely that she could never permit her son to work for people who did not trust him. Actually, as it turned out, he had not stolen any meat that day because the butcher had so little that he hadn't dared!

This touchiness, I believe, was the reason for the frequent changing of jobs among the servants — if they couldn't change anything else, they could at least change employers. To most of the foreigners, this was evidence of mere irresponsibility, but it probably went deeper than that.

The story of Heriberto is a crowning example. Manuela, his wife, who was fat and unattractive, and Felipa, his mother-in-law, scrawny and toothless, worked first for Papa in Torreón and then later in El Paso for me. As they were unprepossessing, unintelligent and spoke no English, they had a hard time making ends meet. Heriberto, on the other hand, did nothing at all. They lived in a tenement on the American side, but on Sundays, all dressed up in their best, they went over to Juárez and walked around the plaza, Heriberto swinging his cane and Manuela clinging delightedly to his arm.

"Why don't you make Heriberto go to work and help support you?" I asked her once in exasperation.

"Oh, no, señora, he couldn't do that!"

"Why not? American men work to support their wives and families, why can't he?"

"Well, you see, señora, he was educated as a merchant and since he has no capital . . ." She shrugged expressively.

During the depression they moved to California, where the job for which Heriberto had been preparing all his life, miraculously presented itself. He became a labor agitator.

There were quite a few independent businessmen in Torreón. Some walked alongside their overloaded burros, crying, "Leña! Leññaaa!" (wood) in a singularly penetrating whine. Others sold water or lemonade, and some sold ice cream which was more like sherbet. One burro carried a small keg with a tin drinking cup chained to it — his owner cried "Agua de Chia." I presume that's the spelling — the product was a milky-looking drink made from some sort of seeds, very sticky and in much demand. I never got to taste it, for Papa vetoed the common drinking cup, if only for esthetic reasons.

The market consisted of little stalls (*puestos*) under a shed—like roof made of *manta,* each one presided over by a man or woman, sometimes an entire family. Each sold one thing; onions, fruit, *aguacates* (avocados), etc. Some offered dishes — *ollas, cazuelas,* and other items made of the thin glazed clay. You could buy lard — a *centavo* purchased about a tablespoonful served up on a bit of newspaper. Another vendor roasted sweet corn over a *brasero.*Women had buckets full of *tortillas* wrapped in (hopefully) clean cloths. Other foods were offered already cooked, the most tempting of which was the *torta compuesta,* the Mexican equivalent of a hamburger "with everything." They smelled simply wonderful and tasted just as good, if you could banish speculations about the origin of the meat, which was apt to be goat, burro, or even, it was said, dog. I wouldn't doubt it in the least, for the town was full of dogs and generally short on meat. And, speaking of meat, we were always careful not to buy meat on Mondays, as it was likely to be the aftermath of the Sunday bullfight and tougher than steel. (Torreón was too small to rate bullfighting of any professional sort until I was a young lady, but Lerdo and Gómez were larger.)

But there was always chicken and turkey. (Did you know that the turkey is so ubiquitous in Mexico that there are twelve different names for it, aside from the Spanish *pavo?*) They ran about loose, saving their owners the necessity of feeding them. Quail were trapped and kept in runs, and the town was full of pigeons. During the Revolution when meat was practically unknown, Papa's cook used to fix him a squab now and then, snatching one from the nests on the roof of the little house in which he was then living. One day when he was sitting out in front a squab fell from one of the nests and landed on the ground. Immediately three large pigeons swooped down and, using beaks and wings, lifted the baby bird back up into the nest. After that Papa refused to eat any more — he said it made him feel like a cannibal.

The market was always a gay place. There was much conversation and laughter whether there were any customers or not — it was amazing how much conversational mileage they could get out of practically nothing.

Mexican households were always huge affairs, involving all sort of relatives, near or distant, prospering or starving together. There were invariably animals of all sorts, cats, dogs, birds, goats. Parrots were special favorites, and old María, who worked for me after I was married, always brought hers to work on her shoulder under her *rebozo,* where it had obviously ridden many times before. It spent the day in our patio screaming and, when opportunity offered, biting us. Songbirds were popular too — canaries, and a little wild bird, rather like a sparrow in size and shape but gay with color and possessed of a sweet little tune, which was trapped and caged.

The Mexicans are a people with much heart, and even the poorest would extend his hospitality to some lost soul, so that frequently you found a peon sharing his hut and meager supply of *tortillas* with some complete stranger, who often remained for life. These were called *arrimados*, derived from the verb *arrimarse*, which means to nestle and then by extension and common practice to mean to cling to, like a barnacle.

Mexican babies were nursed by their mothers until they were about three, unless of course another claimant to the milk arrived in the meantime. Along with this they were fed everything their parents ate, including chile. Which was perfectly natural with the very poor, who were doing well to eat at all. But it obtained even with the well-to-do. After I married, one of our neighbors was a wealthy family with a pair of sickly looking seven or eight months old twins, each with its own *nana*. One day I saw the *nanas* purchase four ears of fresh roasted corn, settle each baby with one, and happily eat one themselves.

Chapter X — OUR FAMILY

W I HAVE MENTIONED before that we were all trilingual, slipping from German to Spanish to English without thinking and frequently using all three tongues in the same sentence. Every language has its own particularly felicitous phrases expressing some special nuance of meaning in a way that no other word can. The word *gemütlich,* for instance, had a sudden vogue some years ago, but to us it was everyday talk, even though we were occasionally called on to explain it to others. Some Spanish words are usually apt, such as *mediopelo,* which means ordinary or common in relation to people, with overtones of gentility. English, of course, has a multitude of such expressions, especially in slang. We used them all, and we developed a sort of language of our own, adding *ed* or *ing* to Spanish infinitives, which confused our hearers no end.

Another confusing thing was the frequency of nicknames in the family — nearly all of us had them. Fidi was the eldest, dark and extraordinarily handsome, and he had been named for Papa. I came next, burdened with the names Tulitas Paulita for two of the aunts. (Tulitas, in case you are curious, is a diminutive, believe it or not, for Gertrude.) When I was very small a nursemaid, fresh off the boat from Sweden, had tried to call me darling. Fidi, two years older than I, had picked it up and as a result I have been called Dalla all my life. Harry (Henry Anthony) was so blond when he was little that his hair scarcely showed — he was called Pelón (Baldy). Alice's name easily shortened to Al. Carlos, the third brother, was nicknamed Bub, which rhymes neither with boob or club, but something in between. A circus that came had a midget, Count Bubelo, who looked exactly like my brother, so we promptly christened him Bubelo and then shortened the name. Robert, the youngest, had the worst luck. His nickname was Chulo, which means dear or sweet, very hard on a little boy after about age six.

Being on the rail line between Mexico City and Juárez, gateway to the United States, Torreón was in a position, despite its smallness, to get some of the best as well as some of the worst entertainment. We heard Tetrazzini, fresh from her triumph in Mexico City, before she took the United States by storm. We also saw some of the corniest "draymas" ever produced. In one plume-and-dagger opus the hero, returning in Act II after twenty years' absence, wore the same bedraggled clothes he had had on Act I. He ran about the stage, holding his cloak up over his nose and his fellow actors obligingly refused to recognize him. Papa growled disgustedly, "How could they fail to recognize that dilapidated feather in his hat?"

Occasionally a group of American hopefuls, having toured Mexico on a shoestring, would arrive wearily wending their way back home. Not infrequently the string would break entirely, and it would take some sort of benefit or subscription to get them out of town.

All Mexican shows had prompters, who had extended their duties until they read *all* the lines before the actors did, making it sound like a bad soundtrack. This got to be such a nuisance that finally some shows advertised as an added attraction that they were "without benefit of prompter."

Sometimes the local Mexicans would put on *tandas*, sketches which were usually very good, since most Mexicans are good actors. Some were musicals in which the "ladies of the town" provided the chorus. Tosca, wife of Papa's youngest brother, Ed, arrived in Torreón with a huge wardrobe of evening dresses. After awhile she decided they were entirely too well known and sold them to an old clothes man. At the next *tanda* the entire chorus was rigged out in Tosca's old ball gowns, much to everybody's amusement.

Papa drew an amusing little sketch of a play he'd seen in which Maximilian was sitting on his throne conferring with one of his generals. It was pouring rain and someone held an umbrella over the Emperor's head while the general, presumably used to hazards in the field, merely dripped.

The walls of the stage were made of that useful material, *manta*, and immediately offstage were the dressing rooms. The lighting consisted of oil lamps or candles, and when they were carried off into the dressing rooms, we had an interesting entr'acte provided by the silhouettes of the cast dressing and undressing.

Other entertainment we dug up ourselves. There were *tertulias*, sort of afternoon dances, given at a pavilion between Torreón and Gómez, where there was a splintery, knotholed platform. Parents brought food, fixing the coffee in big tubs over open fires, and we danced to the music of a local orchestra. We went on horseback rides, the railroad tracks our bridle path. I was not happy about my riding habit, which had been made at home out of the ever-useful *manta* and I was no horsewoman, but I went. Once, however, an approaching train forced us off onto the high bank alongside the rails, and my horse slipped and we rolled down the embankment. I was not hurt, but my enthusiasm diminished considerably.

Most of the time you could walk across the wide sandy bed of the river if you didn't mind dust. But during the summer when the water came down we all had to use the streetcar if we wanted to go to Lerdo or Gómez. Gómez had tennis courts and a baseball diamond, so it was very popular, and Lerdo's Alameda was much larger and more attractive than the plaza in Torreón. These activities were permissible to the foreigners in the afternoon without benefit of chaperon, although usually there were young married couples around anyway. When the bicycle craze hit we rode around town, a very limited operation, since none of the streets was paved, and all had been churned into dust a foot deep. During the night the dust settled, but as time and traffic went on during the day it rose higher and and higher until by sunset there was a regular curtain of it, and people walking along were completely invisible, and a man on a burro gave a strange eerie effect with only his head and shoulders showing. And when the wind blew, which it did frequently, all the topsoil swirled about horribly.

Next door to our house was Papa's office, a very interesting place full of drawing tables and desks and maps and plats. It smelled of ink and metal, and there were great boxes of surveying instruments and other tools of his trade. He employed a German engineer and several draftsmen. One of them, Mr. W., went on periodic binges. The *cocheros,* knowing that he never remembered what happened while he was drinking, took unholy advantage of him, coming to the office and demanding pay for taking him home, whether they had or not. When he sobered up he would work night and day, even going without food sometimes, to catch up. Papa valued him highly, as he was a fine man outside of this one failing, and even told him that if he would abstain from drink for six months he would make him a partner. Mr. W., did this, and the day that the six months was up he took a drink to test his hard-won sobriety. And then, of course, he was off again. Eventually he got to the point where he could no longer work and Papa had to let him go. Papa was constantly hiring draftsmen, and each one stayed through his year's contract and then quit to go into business for himself. Finally in disgust Papa hired two draftswomen from the United

States. One of them stayed through *her* contract and then married one of the ex-draftsmen and went into business with him. The other one stayed till the Revolution started and then went back to New York and became an architect.

Papa was gone a lot of the time, building bridges and dams and things all over Mexico. When he was very young he did a survey of one of the big estates, the Terrazas properties, perhaps. At any rate, it was all desert country with water holes so far apart that they had to flog the mules almost to death to get from one to another. The water holes were nearly all just puddles covered with green scum, which they would brush aside in order to drink. In between times they had to rely on the moisture in cactus plants.

On another surveying trip he was on horseback riding through waist-high brush when a sudden shower came up. Even with a raincoat on he found himself thoroughly drenched. But the peons walking behind him emerged absolutely dry. It developed that when the rain began they had simply stripped, put their clothes in the peaked crowns of their sombreros, and moved along stark naked till the rain was over.

Another time he was measuring a brewery, walking backwards and paying out chain, when suddenly he glanced behind him and saw a great pit. He was too unbalanced to throw himself forward so he had to jump backward to land safely on the other side. Later on he measured the hole and decided that even with a running start he could not have leaped it, so his guardian angel must have been on the job for sure.

Two of his workmen got into a fight when he was building a dam somewhere out in the boondocks, and one knifed the other, wounding him seriously. Papa sent word of what had occurred to the nearest town, asking them to come get the men. The authorities sent word that Papa should bring them in, which he refused to do, since the wounded man was in no condition to ride, and, anyway, Papa didn't have the time. There was a brisk exchange of messages before the authorities got around to sending for the men, and by that time the victim was about well. Which was fortunate, for the soldiers took them both, put the assailant in jail and made the assailee go to work to pay the other man's twenty-five peso fine.

Papa once spent three months in Mexico City, waiting to testify in a big lawsuit over the irrigation water from the Río Nazas. Conscientiously he would go to court every morning to find that the other engineers, or at least some of them, had not bothered to turn up, so he'd go back to the hotel. He was being paid 100 pesos a day, so he finally relaxed about the whole thing and enjoyed his vacation. One night late he was walking along with a friend, who was a little drunk and who insisted that they buy a lottery ticket. They found only one vendor still open and all he had was three quarters of a ticket. The other man refused drunkenly to buy any less than a whole ticket, and Papa, who had been buying lottery tickets for years without any luck, didn't press the issue. As it happened, the vendor had to keep the ticket, which won the 2,000,000 peso Spanish lottery.

All day long we could hear the brewmaster at Papa's brewery bellowing at the other employees, who were scared to death of him. All except Uncle Triny, who was the bookkeeper. Triny was about 5 feet 6 and certainly couldn't have weighed, soaking wet, more than 125 pounds. But he talked right back to Hans, to the delight of the rest of them. Hans may have pulled his punches a little on account of Triny being Papa's brother, but not much, for he had an ungovernable temper and he was a valuable man. The beer he brewed was considered the finest in Mexico and he was getting an unheard of 400 pesos monthly. Written into his contract was his daily quota of ⅛ of a keg of beer and he never missed a drop. After awhile he got so difficult he was driving all the other employees away, so Papa had to let him go. Still later the brewery was forced out of business by some financial shenanigans on the part of other breweries in the area. The Wulffs had many sterling qualities but, except for old Anton, financial wizardry was not among them.

Over the years Papa had employed hundreds and hundreds of men, so when he got into a *coche* in Monterrey and saw how familiar the driver looked, he began racking his brains to try to remember where he'd known the man. Suddenly a man on the street yelled, "Adios, Sardina," and Papa knew immediately where he'd seen him before. In a can.

Living in such a small place with so many nationalities and resultant idiosyncrasies required a good deal of diplomacy, a sort of community broken-field running, for all of us. Papa had a finger in various business pies outside his engineering work, such as the brewery. So for business reasons, if nothing else, he couldn't afford to be too difficult about certain matters. One trying situation cropped up annually when we packed up and returned to San Antonio for our yearly shopping spree. It was a big undertaking, both physically and financially. For one thing, there was no paper money, and just carrying enough silver pesos for the train trip was, literally, a heavy burden. As soon as word got out that we were going, practically everyone in town rushed over with an *encargo*, something they wanted us to buy for them. The range of items was nearly unlimited — stove parts, clothing, books, business stationery, furniture — oh, almost anything you might name. I remember one person who ordered an artificial arm. Later on, after I was married, two patients of Billee's, middle-aged maiden ladies, asked him to bring them a red-haired baby boy for adoption. He did.

We could hardly turn these commissions down, for we had *encargos* of our own when someone else was going, and anyway Papa and Mama were too good-hearted to mind very

An irrigation dam, built by Fred Wulff, is pictured on his office stationery.

Torreón se transforma por la recia voluntad de sus hombres!...

HONOR A LA INICIATIVA

PREMIO AL TRABAJO

PERSEVERANCIA

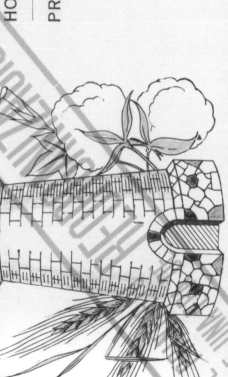

En el año de 1850 el Sr. Don Pedro Santacruz construyó el Torreón primitivo, dando origen al nombre que hoy ostenta. En este mismo año se empezó a formar el Rancho del Torreón, que al principio estuvo compuesto simplemente de una casa destinada a albergar primero, al constructor y después a los sucesivos administradores de la Presa del Torreón, que con sus cambios y reformas se convirtió en la hoy Presa del Coyote. La Presa así como la gran extensión territorial que iba a irrigar eran propiedad de Don Leonardo Zuloaga, señor feudal de positivas energías a quien corresponde

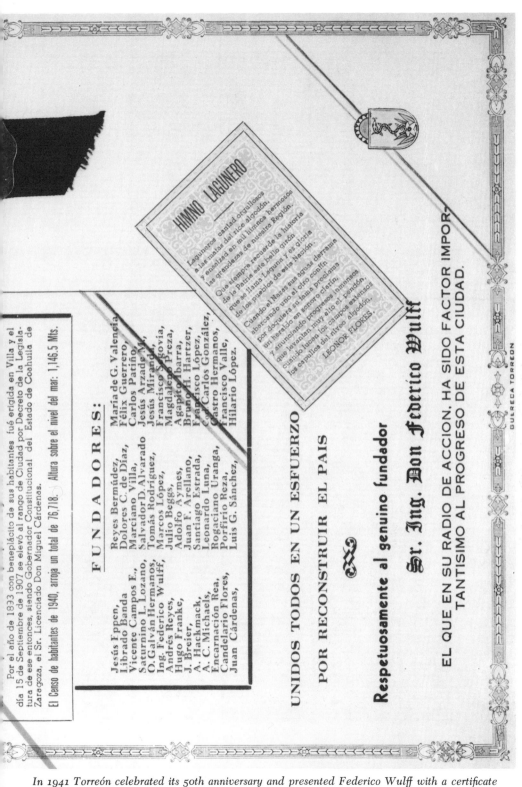

In 1941 Torreón celebrated its 50th anniversary and presented Federico Wulff with a certificate as the principal founding father. He had laid out the city in the early 1880's. By 1941 it was the fourth largest city in Mexico.

Torreón main street as it looked in 1906

much. But there were times when they were about ready to give up. In those days ladies' hats were large and rode boldly on top of knots or pompadours well bolstered by rats and switches and lots of bone hairpins. The question of fit or becomingness did not arise. Once, among other things, three women asked Mama to bring back hats for them. In San Antonio she found that the vogue was for large white hats topped with black birds, so she picked out three of those, taking care to see that each one was slightly different. But she felt such flamboyance was inappropriate for the mother of six children so she bought herself a modest brown one. Later on it got back to her that the ladies were dissatisfied with her choices.

"You notice," pointed out one lady nastily, "that she bought herself a *brown* one."

The biggest trouble was that there were always some people who wanted to do it on the cuff, which posed a problem when we were rather short ourselves, and occasionally one or two wanted permanent credit, you might say. After being stung a few times Papa stopped buying things if he didn't have the money in hand. To one deadbeat who had the nerve to upbraid him for not bringing his *encargo*, Papa explained smoothly, "Well, you see, before I left for San Antonio I wrote down each item on a slip of paper and then put the money I'd been given for it on top of the slip. Unluckily, the window was open and a little breeze sprang up and blew away all the slips that were not weighted down with pesos."

Chapter XI — CHARACTERS

❧ PERHAPS BECAUSE it took a certain amount of non con-
formity in the system to pull up stakes and settle down in a
foreign land, the transplants were mostly individual, and
some of them were very definitely characters. Even a good
many of the transient visitors were on the oddball side, including one Canadian woman, otherwise rather ordinary, who
flatly refused to believe that only the bad women of the town
went out on the streets during the *siesta* hour. She persisted
in going out and nearly involved her brother, whom she was
visiting, in a number of fights as a result. Another was a young
Frenchman, who claimed to belong to a cadet branch of the
De La Rochefoucald family, who used to take his typewriter
down into the street, sit on the curb and get out his invoices
under the somewhat brighter rays of the street light.

One of the most unusual and delightful persons among the
permanent residents of the Laguna area was Mrs. Potter,
wife of the assistant manager of Hacienda Tlahualilo, which
is worth mentioning for its own sake. This place was about
sixty kilometers from Torreón. It belonged to an English
company and was at one time said to be the largest cotton
plantation in the world. Besides cotton they raised enormous
quantities of wheat, sorghum, and other grains. In order to
facilitate the work, there were little clusters of adobe houses,
called *ranchos,* dotted about the *hacienda's* many acres, to
which the laborers moved, bag and baggage, wives and children, when the work to be done was in that area. Later on the

company set up its own school system. The management also gave each laborer a small plot of ground on which he could raise whatever he liked. A great many chose to raise watermelons, for which there was a brisk market in Torreón and vicinity, and during the summer months two boxcars of watermelons left the place daily, the company marketing them and turning the proceeds back to the workers. Hacienda Tlahualilo had its own doctor and, eventually, a little hospital, pretty well equipped, staffed by a Mexican nurse whom they had sent to El Paso for training.

All the crops were raised by irrigation, and there was a huge system of canals, the main canal being the size of a river with banks wide enough for two cars abreast. It was really a lovely place, with great cottonwood trees growing along the canal banks and much greenery around the cluster of houses where the management lived.

Just outside the gates of the *hacienda* was a little town, called Zaragosa, complete with *jefe*, stores, bowling alley, a church and of course several *cantinas*. Later on, when motion pictures came in they had an outdoor cinema. The *gente* (that is, the Mexicans) sat on the right side of the screen, and the managerial force sat on the other, requiring them to read the subtitles mirror fashion. When talkies came in, the cinema was moved to a big adobe building with little or no ventilation. One sat on very hard benches, generally rather splintery, and tried to hold one's breath. The man who ran it spoke no English and it didn't bother him if the soundtrack got off and the heroine suddenly began talking in a deep bass voice, but the audience would start stamping its feet until the matter was corrected.

The bowling alley was deeply grooved so that if you caught the groove you could make a strike every time. There was also a sign on the wall, in Spanish: PLEASE PARK YOUR GUNS BEFORE BOWLING. It seems that a Mexican army officer got shot in the foot when his gun fell out of his holster when he was bowling.

The residents of the town worked at the *hacienda* and sometimes doubled in brass, with businesses of their own. The barber, for instance, ran one of the combines during the month of the wheat harvest, and during that time not only labor but management too got very shaggy indeed.

The management, mostly Britishers and Canadians with a sprinkling of Americans, lived a very leisurely life, working in the morning only. After the *siesta* came tennis or golf and then tea at someone's house and dinner at eight or nine at night. There was a great deal of entertaining back and forth between the different houses, and conversational topics got rather battered with much use.

At Christmas the manager usually gave a big dinner for the whole colony, with guests from Torreón, Lerdo, and other places. Thanksgiving dinner belonged to the Potters and other holiday occasions were distributed among the rest. Usually someone or several someones had houseguests, and the man-woman ratio was agreeably bolstered by a number of young men, since the United States government had an entomological station there for the study of the pink bollworm and other cotton pests. The bachelors lived at the Mess, which was presided over by Mrs. Vaughn, widow of an early manager and head of the school system, and the Mess took its turn at entertaining too.

Jane Potter was considerably older than I, though not yet Mama's age, and she was very beautiful, played the piano well and ran the social life of the colony. She was pretty domineering and many a guest found himself playing bridge whether he liked it or not. She traded on her age horribly, and any criticism of her playing — she wasn't very good at it — invariably brought forth, "You can't talk to an old lady like me that way, young man." But she was always kind and the poor people always knew that she would help them if they needed it. Periodically she got up entertainments to raise money for some of the needier ones, and when she traveled to the United States every year she always took time to go to the ten-cent store and pick up a lot of spectacles for those whose eyesight was failing. She would stand there and try them on to get varying degrees of strength in the lenses.

She also had a finger in various other pies. For instance, one of the stenographers in the company office was a woman who had for years supported a large family of brothers and sisters, who were not in the least appreciative, although she had given up marriage to help them. Through one of the Lonely Hearts magazines she had begun a correspondence with an American sailor, and he finally asked her to marry him.

Such an uproar as there was! It wasn't nice or ladylike or the sort of thing a decent young Mexican woman would do, and the poor woman was besieged on all sides by relatives, friends, and so on. Finally in tears she came to Mrs. Potter. Jane had the man investigated, found he was a respectable person who probably would make a good husband. So she helped the woman make up her mind, helped her buy a trousseau, and sent her to the States to meet and marry the man. I was then living in El Paso, Texas, and Jane wrote me that the woman was coming through, so I did my best to help her on her way. The marriage was a long and happy one, and years later the son of the marriage, who was on one of the nuclear subs, stopped off in El Paso to see me, a fine young man.

Jane herself had come from a good family in New York, I believe, and at sixteen had gone as governess to the children of a Spanish count living in Guatemala. The count and countess had made her one of the family, and she traveled with them when they went to Europe. When she fell in love with a handsome mining engineer named Harry Potter, the countess furnished her with a Paris trousseau, trunks and trunks of it.

Whereupon Harry took her to Mexico to a village at the foot of a large, commanding mountain and settled her in a small adobe house. Then he got on a mule and went up the mountain several hundred or thousand feet to the mine he managed. Jane stood the separation about a week — then she got a mule of her own and rode up to the mine, where she discovered Harry living, like the rest of the personnel, in a cave. Over his vociferous objections she moved in and settled down. She even sent away for wallpaper and papered the walls of the cave with her own hands.

There was quite a self-sufficient little colony up there, including a company store and a bakery. However, after watching the bakers, who worked naked due to the heat, patting off their sweat with the dough they were kneading, Jane started baking her own bread.

After she had been there about a month she had her first visitors. These were a man, his wife and two daughters, who lived at another mine on another mountain some hours distant by horseback. The real purpose of the visit, it developed after several hours of tea and conversation, was for mama and the girls to see Jane's trousseau. They had heard about it some time before, but had not dared to come to look until they had made themselves riding habits — complete with divided skirt and derby — after the latest style in the chief fashion magazine of the time.

In Tlahualilo the Potters lived in a big cool adobe house with seven servants and half a dozen fox terriers. There were hinged dog doors cut into most of the doors in the house and the dogs ran in and out at will. But they were well behaved — any pet of Jane's was bound to be. The only untoward incident occurred when she played the piano. It was painful to the ears of Chico, the small terrier, and he would howl and rush outside. Whereupon the largest dog would sit close to Jane at the piano, as if to reassure her.

She was the most hospitable soul in the world and was constantly inviting friends and relatives and friends of friends for visits, but she had never been inclined to suffer fools gladly, and as she got older and her arthritis grew worse, she was sometimes apt to be a little snappish with her guests. I recall one woman — a friend of a friend — whom Jane invited, sight unseen, to break her journey to Mexico City at Tlahualilo. Mrs. X turned out to be one of those compulsive braggarts who never let anyone else get a word in edgewise and who claim to be on first-name terms with all the great and near great. She talked about her brother until we decided that if he weren't president of Harvard he certainly ought to be, and she was full of some recent archaeological discoveries in Mexico, talking as if she had been the finder's closest confidante. (But she never mentioned her husband once!) Jane stood it pretty well, even when the people who came to tea began drifting off before their usual time, but finally the end came. Jane knew all about the discoveries, had entertained the archaeologist, and with several incisive questions she reduced the woman to a quivering mass of repentant honesty, admitting that she had read about the findings in a magazine and, among other things, that her brother was a dentist somewhere in the Middle West.

One of Jane's illusions was that she could paint. She had studied with someone in Paris for six months when she'd been there with the countess, and she did have an extraordinary gift for catching a likeness. What she needed was a course in anatomy. She had a little studio fixed up at the hacienda, and she painted on my portrait for year whenever I visited there. Finally she finished it and sent it to me, a full length portrait some four feet high and framed in a heavy gold frame. The face was unmistakably mine, but somewhere the rest of me had been lost — I was six inches shorter and many pounds fatter, with a long waist and short legs. My arms were gracefully bent in the picture, but if they had been allowed to swing free they would have reached my knees, and my feet looked like shoes filled with sand. Knowing she might be coming through El Paso, I had to hang the thing in my bedroom where I could wince at it first thing every morning. When she did come she was openly upset that I had not hung it in the living room. I muttered something feeble about not liking to have my portrait hung in full view.

Jane, bless her heart, was a strong character, and like all such, she managed to override and antagonize a lot of people, but her heart was in the right place.

Another character at Tlahualilo was Joe Askew, who had been, according to legend, almost everything — miner, Texas Ranger, etc. I do know that he was a miner, for he came to Torreón in that capacity, and that he drove the stage from Kingston, New Mexico, to Nutt during the gold rush. He came from Sulphur Springs, Texas and was about 5 feet 3 inches, a stocky little man with a round bald head — he always had his hair shaved off — a sense of humor, an excellent mind, no formal education, and a vast curiosity about everything. One elbow had been shattered by a bullet, so he had trouble tying his tie, and a couple of bullets had pierced his abdomen without, however, impairing either his appetite or his digestion. True to the code of the old West, Joe never said anything derogatory about a woman, but he spoke freely to and about men. He spent thirty years in Mexico and never learned any Spanish beyond first-person singular, present tense, but at the *hacienda* where he was in charge of the livestock (concocting bucketsful of horrible smelling messes to dose sick cows and ailing mules) the laborers all knew, loved and understood him. Once, though, a new peon cropped up and Joe wanted him to go to the post office and pick up a parcel.

"Voy a correo, traigo paquete," he said, which translated as "I'm going to the post office, I'll bring a package."

The Mexican said nothing and Joe repeated his request. When nothing happened Joe said angrily, "These dad-blamed Messicans don't even understand their own dad blamed language," adding loudly, "VOY A CORREO, TRAIGO PAQUETE."

The peon, deciding that something was called for, murmured courteously in Spanish, "I hope you have a nice trip."

One time when Joe was returning from the United States he forgot his passport, but insisted airily that he didn't need it — after all he'd lived in Mexico for thirty years. The Mexican immigration inspector said, "I'm sorry, señor, but no man who has lived in Mexico that long could possibly speak Spanish so badly."

During the Revolution, Villa kidnaped Joe, thinking he had Tom Fairbairn, the manager, and hoping that the great English company would pay well for such a valuable employee. Joe disillusioned Villa, who then decided that Fairbairn might pay well for his friend. He instructed Joe to write Tom a letter. He did. It read:

"Dear Tom: Everything is bully. Don't you pay them a damn cent. Joe."

During the interval of waiting Joe undertook to teach the *villistas* the gentle art of playing poker and by the time Tom's answer came back — in the negative — Joe owned all the saddles, guns and other portable property in the entire outfit. Villa then asked Joe to stay on as a member of the band, but when Joe refused, Villa let him go. P.S. Joe had returned his winnings.

Later in life Joe began to lose his eyesight, and for a time he was very depressed about it. But his natural optimism asserted itself, and when I talked to him about it, he said, "It don't matter. I seen plenty in my day."

Chapter XII

HIGH SCHOOL AND AFTER

ᛞ WHEN I WAS THIRTEEN I was sent back to San Antonio to go to high school. Fidi had already gone and was at the Seeley Academy, but I was to stay with Tante Lit and Uncle Nep and go to Main Avenue High. They had a lovely house and plenty of help and it was pleasant living there.

Uncle Nep was an Austrian whose father had been an officer in the Austrian army. He had been killed in battle, leaving a wife and five sons. The government educated the boys, most of whom were very handsome. One, in fact, was so spectacularly good-looking that Emperor Franz Josef ordered him to court just for the pleasure of looking at him. Uncle Nep was not handsome, but he had a way with him, saying flattering things and constantly bringing home gifts and flowers.

I found the adjustment difficult at first. Everything was so different — even Tante Lit and Uncle Nep, acting *in loco parentis,* were different. School was such a change — so many pupils, so many girls, all seeming so much more sure of themselves and more sophisticated than I. Even Ida, my old friend, had changed. (I had too, naturally, but with the myopia of adolescence that never occurred to me.) And I was awfully homesick. My grades suffered as a result and I barely scraped through that first year.

Only one incident of that time comes back to me, largely as a view of the customs of that period. A scapegrace Groos cousin from Germany had come to San Antonio, and Tante Lit was going to take him for a drive. She wanted me to go along too, since it was not proper for a married woman to go driving alone with a man. (The coachman, Robert, who had worked for them for years, was there, but as a chaperon he did not count.) I agreed reluctantly, if I could be allowed to get out at Ida's house, and I insisted that they go there first. That made my chaperonage very brief indeed and I suppose, properly speaking, she should have curtailed the drive then and there. But she didn't, and I never found out whether her reputation suffered as a result.

Uncle Nep went broke and they left San Antonio for Torreón to stay with Mama and Papa, so that the other two years (high school was only three years then) I spent with Tante Carrie and Uncle Conrad Goeth in their big red brick house on Adams Street. He was a lawyer, doing very well, and there were two children, Fred, several years younger than I, and Arthur, still younger. Tante Lotts lived with them too.

Gradually my confidence grew. I acquired boy friends — one, especially, who didn't mind carrying my books the two miles home every afternoon. Some of the boys we went around with were students at the West Texas Military Academy, and our dances were held at the Armory. I even had a part in a play. I was supposed to be the French maid, wearing a chic little black dress with a ruffled apron and a dab of ruffle for a cap. It was a very small part, but since my *vis-a-vis* was one of the cutest boys in school I was perfectly happy. But one of the other girls had an eye on him, and through some skullduggery (and my own naiveté) I suddenly found myself playing a bigger part opposite the most unattractive boy in the cast.

This was the Gibson Girl era, and we looked at Charles Dana Gibson's drawings and wished that we could look as serene, as beautiful, as poised as the women he depicted.

We certainly tried hard. For one thing, the Gibson Girl, when she wore a shirtwaist and skirt, always managed to keep the waist of her skirt high up in the back, almost half way to her shoulder blades. Hers was done with a stroke of the pen — when we followed suit, it meant anchoring the waistband with large safety pins to our corsets, no mean job. We struggled mightily with our hair to get the right forward thrust to our pompadours. I was generally in despair about my hair, for this was also the era of the Seven Sutherland Sisters (with hair hanging to the hems of their dresses), and I felt as if I were practically bald because mine only came about halfway down to my elbows. Nightly I rolled it up on bits of paper and used rats and switches to give it the thickness it lacked — the only thing I liked about it was the color, a nice golden brown. How times change! Now, sixty odd years later even I have to have my hair cut and thinned.

I did pretty well in most of my subjects, but my favorite was math, probably partly because I was the only girl along with several boys in the advanced math class. We took German from a young man who was new at teaching and had the horrible disadvantage of blushing. When we read some of the more romantic passages in Goethe we used to clasp our hands and sigh, "Oh Herr Schultz, isn't that romantic?" and the poor man would color to the roots of his hair and look ready to rush out of the room.

Fidi had graduated from Seeley the year before and was admitted to the University of Texas, but on condition because he was only fifteen. I graduated myself at sixteen. My dress was lovely, made with hundreds of tiny pleats, and I received as many bouquets as any other girl. (No one gave graduation gifts, just bouquets of flowers.)

Meanwhile down in Torreón things were happening. Papa was building a house halfway up the hill we had climbed that

first morning. Some company, a brewery, I think, had dug
the basement and built the three-foot rock walls and then
gone broke. Papa had bought the thing with an eye to giving
it to Uncle Henry to use for some business or other. When
Mama found that out she had a fit, because the one real bone
of contention in the family was the constant help Papa kept
giving his brothers and sisters. The Wulff fortune had vanished, and Grandma Wulff, whose big interest had always
been her five girls, according to a possibly apocryphal story,
made Henry and Triny promise not to marry until the re-
maining girls, Lula and Maria, did. Just why they didn't is
a mystery — they were both attractive and pretty. One story
is that Lula turned down the man she wanted because it was
considered proper then to turn down a man twice before
accepting his proposal. Her beloved apparently didn't know
the ground rules and left town. Her brother-in-law, hearing
the tale, offered to fetch him back, but she felt that would be
too unwomanly and forward. Whatever the story, she spent
the rest of her long life with good works, a wonderful sense
of humor, and not much else. Maria, I think, was just too
prudish. I know that years later when I suggested she visit
a chiropodist she was horrified. "Let a man see my feet!"

At any rate Mama had wanted a house of her own all these
years and she decided that the side of the hill was just the
place for it. So Papa built a modified Rhenish castle of gray
stone, and it was a lovely house. Of course, the location had
some disadvantages, although the view was marvelous. They
spent a year digging a well and got salty water, but by that
time the city had a water system, so they hooked onto that
and used the well for watering the grounds and filling the
swimming pool. Another disadvantage was the eighty-one
steps that led up to the house — wide, shallow, with flat places
in between, but still an awful lot of steps. At the foot of the

hill Papa built an office, a two-story building. The house, despite its Germanic overtones, was promptly christened Chalet Wulff.

During this time Papa had been struggling with the same old problem of educating the rest of the family, and Tante Lit, who was very independent, felt keenly that she should in some way repay Mama and Papa's hospitality. She offered to take the lot of us to Oakland, California, so that Fidi and I could attend the University of California and the younger ones could go to grade and high school. She rented a big two-story wooden house. In San Antonio I couldn't even attend my graduation ball — I had to change my clothes and get right on the train for the West Coast, clutching the most cherished of my bouquets.

The first problem we ran into out there was help. As soon as an applicant answered our ad and heard that there were seven in the family, she immediately bowed out. So we finally hit on the idea of saying that there were only four in the family. Fidi was to live at his fraternity house temporarily, Harry was farmed out, and I stayed with a friend. The next applicant was a Chinaman, and he decided to stay. He would say, "How many foh dinnah tonight, Mis Lonse? Foh?", and she would say, "Oh, no, tonight there'll be five." And then six, and finally the whole family had been infiltrated back into the fold. And as we had hoped, he liked us and stayed on.

For all this Papa was sending 400 dollars a month — the exchange was two for one. Fidi got a big portion of it, for his expenses at college were high. He belonged to a good fraternity and had gotten in with a very wealthy group. At seventeen he was dating one of the senior girls. Since he was very handsome and serious, looking older than his years, she had no trouble accepting him as a contemporary until one of the San Antonio cousins, visiting out there, let the cat out of the bag, and she dropped him like a hot potato.

I had intended to go to the university too, but at that time there was a campaign on by the boys to get rid of the coeds, and there was much throwing of ink and other such things, so Fidi thought it better for me not to go there. I went instead to the Hopkins Art Institute in San Francisco, going across on the ferry every day and feeling very daring and adventurous. China painting was the vogue then, and I had three lessons a week in that and a lesson or two in drawing and water color. I met some boys and girls, and struck up a friendship with a girl named Rose, who was considered rather daring because she was taking a full art course and planned to go to Paris to study. With my ideas of Paris conditioned by novels I had read secretly about artists, I was flattered and not a little frightened by Rose's friendship.

One day she suggested we meet for lunch, adding, "I'll be in life class and might be delayed, so just come in and wait for me."

I hadn't the remotest idea what life class might be, so after I finished with the violets I was putting on a saucer I cleaned up, put on my hat, and walked briskly down the hall to the room Rose had indicated, pulled aside the heavy brown curtain over the doorway and walked in. The first thing I saw was a man, naked except for a G string, standing on a platform in the middle of the room. I nearly fainted. Why I was so shocked I don't know — I had bathed my little brothers, and all the peon children went without diapers or drawers up to about the age of four. I managed to make it through lunch somehow, but after that I let my friendship with Rose quietly fade away.

All of us took the move in stride except Robert, aged four, who flatly refused to speak any English, although he was glib enough in Spanish and German. Finally he was goaded into it by one of the other kids, and turned out to be just as fluent. It was during this period, I think, that he got a "thing" about noses, commenting very freely and usually adversely about every one he saw. An old family friend who had a huge nose was coming to visit and we threatened the direst consequences if Robert even so much as mentioned the word. When the man appeared he had a red beard that reached halfway down his chest. Robert took one look, then sidled over to me and whispered, "What about the beard?"

During the time we were there the exchange suddenly went to three to one. We hadn't exactly been living in the lap of luxury, but now we had to economize further. The children had been getting five cents a week spending money, and they were allowed to go downtown on Saturdays to spend this magnificent sum. Now, however, they had to make a choice between the ice cream and the streetcar home.

A welcome break for me was the visit of Don Evaristo Madero, father of Francisco and Papa's good friend, with his daughters Barbara and María, just about my age. They were going to the wine country to see a friend of his, and I was invited to go along. I was very stylish with a train to my suit skirt, and Don Evaristo fussed at the girls for not wearing clothes like mine, when actually they were much more sensibly dressed. We drove out to the vineyards in a carriage, and I was fascinated by the sight of those great clusters of grapes growing on what looked like little hills of vines, instead of in an arbor as I had always seen them before. The Maderos found the traffic in San Francisco rather frightening and when the girls would hesitate on the curb, the old man would say, "*Andale!* Here you do not walk, you run." But the pace finally got him down too, and he insisted on leaving just when the girls were getting into their stride. He said, "Here in this country there are too many 'arriopas'." When I asked what he meant he explained, "All the time they are saying to me, 'Harry op, Papa, you are too slow'."

At the end of six months Mama came out to take us back,

probably on account of the expense. Fidi remained, moving into his fraternity house. Tante Lit, with a sigh of relief, relinquished us and went to San Antonio for a visit.

Mama wasn't well and how she ever endured the trip out with her tendency to car sickness, I don't know. On the way back she developed, in addition, a habit of fainting at odd moments.

That put me in charge of things. I was seventeen and probably should have had a good deal more capacity and poise than I did, but I'd been brought up in Mexico and my few excursions into the greater freedom of the United States had been well guarded and supervised. I'd never really been on my own in my life before, and the prospect of taking a sick woman and four children from San Francisco to Torreón scared me to death.

Uncle Charlie Groos, Mama's brother, and his wife put us on the train in San Francisco, and I was dismayed to find the Pullman entirely empty. Then a couple got on, and I brightened up so visibly that my aunt leaned over and whispered, "Don't count on any help from that woman. She's running away with another woman's husband."

The couple vanished into the stateroom and we never saw their faces again.

It was January, and since neither San Francisco nor Torreón ever had much real winter weather, it did not occur to us that it might turn cold. We were on the Santa Fe and at each station where there was a Harvey House we had to rush the whole caboodle out and feed them. Harry was a great help, but he was only fifteen, and besides he and I had to take care of Mama, helping her out at every stop and walking her along the platform so she wouldn't faint. (I don't know whose idea this rather heroic method of treatment was — certainly in retrospect it seems it would have been better to let her rest on the train and if she was going to faint, let her do it in comfort.) In Albuquerque there was a foot of snow on the ground and more falling. The kids, who had seen very little snow in their lives, were enchanted, and it was a struggle to get them away from this strange stuff and into the dining room. Alice, who was twelve, was capable of helping them order, while Harry and I took turns grabbing a bite, then rushing back to Mama with whatever we thought she could eat, walking her and then one of us had to pay the bill for the children and see that they got back on the train. I was so nervous I couldn't eat.

There were further complications at Albuquerque. We had to change trains, and we found that some mistake had been in the reservations, which had been wired for, and instead of the stateroom and compartment we were counting on, there were only two uppers. A very kind man, seeing our predicament and probably noting the tears in my eyes, gave us his lower and spent the night in the men's lavatory. We put Mama and Robert in the lower, Harry and Bub in one upper, and Alice and I took the other. I was so shaken that I dared not undress, feeling as if such relaxation might bring on fresh disasters, and I wouldn't even let Alice take off her shoes. When she complained I slapped her and said, "You're lucky I let you take off your hat."

Somehow we got through the rest of the trip — providentially, perhaps, the remainder is blurred in my memory. I don't think I ever really appreciated Papa until I saw him on the station platform.

Chapter XIII — DEBUT

W EVEN THOUGH it was only 7:00 A.M., very early for that very leisurely time and place, two good-looking young men were walking up and down the platform. Suddenly Papa was bringing them over and introducing them. "Dr. Jamieson, Mr. Fairbairn." If I had had any idea that I was looking at my future husband and his best-man-to-be, I might have felt differently. As it was, I was thoroughly irritated that Papa, with paternal blindness, had been stupid enough to introduce anybody when I was so wrinkled, dirty and generally awful-looking.

I acknowledged the introduction as pleasantly as I could and then hurried the family into a *coche* and home. When I fussed, Papa laughed and said, "I thought you'd like to meet the two newest bachelors in town. Tom Fairbairn is manager of the soda-water factory and Dr. Jamieson is another Canadian. Both nice young men. They heard you were coming and came down to the station purposely to see you."

I groaned and he laughed again. But I'm sure Mama understood.

Looking at today's teen-agers and their various forms of revolt, I wonder a little at myself at that age. Maybe I wasn't the stuff of which rebels are made. Besides, we had been brought up to respect adults, if for nothing more than sheer staying power in a world where death and illness and hardship were close and familiar things. If we went wrong, it was our fault, not our parents'. We had no ideas about trying to change the world with semantics or revolution or flower power. All we were expected to do was try our very best in our own particular spot. Moreover, we all looked forward to growing up. Adults ran the world, their decisions were listened to, and they had a lot of privileges to which we aspired.

It had been pretty hard to leave my boy friend in San Antonio, but I hadn't questioned the decision that sent me out to California. Out there his memory had been overlaid by the faces of other young men, Fidi's friends, *college* men. But there had been none among them special enough to command my heart, so I hadn't objected at all to coming back to Torreón, even though I knew I would be losing a lot of the freedom I'd had. I liked being home again, in familiar surroundings among familiar and well-loved people. (Hearing again the music of the little street bands made me realize just how much I'd missed that.) It was rather heady to realize that I was now a young lady, ready for marriage, who would be going to balls and dancing with men who, whether they had matrimony in mind or not, were at least matrimonial material — that is, out of school and on their own. Marriage was the only career for a girl in those days, and one unmarried by the age of twenty-five was considered an old maid.

Torreón had grown quite a lot, outstripping Gómez and Lerdo and assuming, in a minor fashion, some of the aspects of a city. There was a magnificent new casino, the walls decorated with huge mirrors and windows hung with marvelous draperies, all imported from France at staggering cost. There was a parquet floor which had cost 10,000 pesos. The ballroom was furnished with lovely light furniture (we would call it fruitwood now), and a fine grand piano. There were other rooms too, equally as fine, a bar and cardrooms, where men foregathered and women were not invited.

There was a city water system, as I have mentioned, and a city sanitary department to take Narciso's place, but since there were no sewers, the same old methods were used. Tosca was a gay, witty woman who dominated slow amiable Uncle Ed completely. One night shortly after they arrived in Torreón she heard a noise outside and got up, conscious of a dreadful odor. The sanitation department at work. She called out. "Who are you?"

The men's English was limited, but one knew enough American slang to tell her succinctly just who they were.

She gave a little scream and rushed back into the bedroom and shook Ed awake. "That man insulted me," she cried. "You've got to do something."

Ed pulled himself together and, realizing by the pervading smell just what was happening, asked, "Just what did he say to you?"

Blushing, she told him, and Ed for once refused to jump at his wife's command.

"That, my dear, is just exactly what it is," he said and turned over and went back to sleep.

The poorer classes still had no sanitary facilities at all and no qualms about relieving themselves wherever they happened to be. When Papa built the big house he also built a warehouse and office for himself at the bottom of the hill. The wall of the warehouse had been whitewashed, and the city, becoming self-conscious, wrote there in foot high letters, "Se prohibe urinarse en esta pared." ("It is forbidden to urinate on this wall.")

Torreón had an Alameda now, a big park on the other side of town, although it wasn't much to see yet because the trees were still small. Beyond it lay the Chinese gardens, a big area where an increasing number of Orientals grew fine vegetables and fruit, thereby incurring the hatred of some of the Mexicans who were not as thrifty or as hard-working. There were more stores and businesses, some even had plate glass windows. There was a Chinese steam laundry. Heretofore there had been only one church, the Catholic Church, but now there was at least one Protestant minister, and Mrs. DaCosta, a devout Episcopalian, had set up a little chapel and every few months she would pay the expenses of the clergyman from Eagle Pass to come down and hold communion services. There were several good restaurants, particularly Sternau's, which had imported foods and even occasional imported items, such as glassware. The men all went there at noon for conversation and a glass of beer or a drink before coming home to the big midday meal at 1:30 or 2:00. The German Club was one of the favorite places for entertainment, including bowling.

Sartorially, too, Torreón had taken a big leap forward. For dress wear the men wore frock coats, just as they always had. But the two young Canadians, at the first ball to which they were invited, had electrified the community by appearing in the first tail coats ever seen there. The next day the tailor was dithering happily over the fact that he had twenty-four orders for such coats.

The women, of course, kept up much better with the fashions, rushing over every time anyone returned from the United States or elsewhere. A long gap between returnees or visitors would leave us way behind, and we would discover, to our chagrin, that while we were still blousing our hair out in front, fashion was now blousing hers out in back. And there would be a big changeover.

Perhaps the most startling change was the advent of the sheath gown. Skirts had been gored but plenty full enough at the bottom for at least one petticoat. The sheath gown was long and tight, so tight that it had to be split so one could walk in it. When the first one appeared in Torreón the whisper, "She has no petticoat on," swooped around the town like a demented bumblebee. The glimpse of ankle afforded by the split was reckoned as a direct invitation to rape or murder or both. But like all styles, it was eventually accepted.

Which reminds me that my granddaughter, who majored in drama at college, can not only paint flats but make them, wielding a hammer with force and skill. She can run a light-board, change sets, make costumes, repair furniture, do almost anything necessary for an amateur production. All in dirty slacks, T shirt and sneakers. Now, in Torreón we had theatricals too, and on the day after my return I was invited to assist in decorating the stage for a show that the bachelors were putting on. I arrived clad in a pale blue satin dress with a slight train and a white panne velvet poke bonnet with a huge red rose under the brim. I don't recall what I was supposed to contribute in the way of help — perhaps move a vase — but at any rate none of the young men objected to the way I looked.

Among the Mexicans everything was very formal, and every new young man was forced to invent reasons for calling on a young lady. Once when we had a New Year's reception a young man from Monterrey was brought by his cousin. He was a very grand young man who sported fine mustachios, spats, and a gold-headed cane. He and the cousin remained long after everyone else departed, and when they finally did leave, I discovered that he had forgotten his cane. I was so naive that I sent the *mozo* after him with it, and he blandly sent it back, saying he would come for it himself.

There were picnics, but we usually had to send out an advance party to find a tree under which we could sit. One of the big *haciendas* had a stand of giant fig trees, and sometimes we were invited there.

On Sunday afternoons we went to the plaza and walked around arm in arm with our beaux (this deviation from the norm was permitted the foreigners). There were *tamaladas* at the pavilion or elsewhere. But no matter where we went we were always well chaperoned, for there was so little to do that all the young married couples, if not the parents, were on hand for all the functions.

One thing we did have plenty of was men — there were dozens of unmarried men and very few girls. No girl, however unattractive, ever had an empty dance card, and the young matrons always had a ball too, both literally and figuratively.

Three young men formed a club, called the Buttinsky Club, to follow me about and horn in on any young man who was paying me attention, even riding over to Lerdo on the streetcar when I had a date to walk in the Alameda there. It was flattering, but did not go over well with the other young men. One of my beaux, a shy young German, used to buy bunches of violets (for a peso you could buy a bunch the size of a dinner plate) and hang them on the doorknob, then ring the bell and rush across the street to hide and see whether I answered the door myself. Battersby, an attractive Englishman, arrived one day in time to see this performance. When he came in he handed me the violets.

Later the German asked him, "Did you gif my flowers to Miss Wulff?"

Battersby nodded. "She was very glad to get them."

The German smiled happily, then as an afterthought inquired, "Did you tell her that I haf brought them?"

"Of course not. I told her I brought them myself."

The wealthy Mexicans entertained lavishly and beautifully. One party was given at the *hacienda* of a member of the Luján family. A special train took the guests from Torreón, and when we disembarked at the end of the railroad spur there were men stationed at intervals with flaming torches to light our way to the house. This was very large and wonderfully decorated — the whole enormous patio adorned with thousands of gardenias wired to every branch and twig. The fragrance was almost overpowering. We danced all night — there was plenty of fine food, wine and two orchestras imported from Mexico City. At six the next morning the train returned us to Torreón.

Another party was at the Cárdenas ranch. The house was simply huge — there were four pianos, just for ordinary wear, you might say. Included in the entertainment was an amateur bullfight, and the Mexican men showed off gallantly, although they were only working with calves. My brother Bub, who was then about twelve, had been trying to buy a horse and had been allowed to go out to the various ranches nearby to look over the stock. He had a friendly, nice personality, and everywhere he went they had taken an interest in him and, among other things, had taught him to rope. At the Cárdenas party he was very much in demand for roping the calves when they got out of hand.

One great point of difference between the Mexicans and the Americans was that the Mexicans were keyed to Continental Europe. They sent to Paris rather than New York for their clothes; their sons and, less frequently, their daughters were educated in France, and French was often a second language. All this, of course, pertained to the upper classes, but the Latin idea that wives are made for childbearing while husbands are free to roam had penetrated to lower levels, and many Mexican girls' highest ambition was to marry a German or American or Englishman. Not that they were necessarily so virtuous, but they usually didn't take the marriage vows with their fingers crossed. On the whole, the Germans did the best job of it — other foreigners found the infiltration of in-laws very irritating, since frequently some or even all of her family moved in with the newlyweds.

The evening parties were always late starting, and Papa, who got very tired of taking me to parties, would always go outside to look at the sky and hope for rain (a very vain hope since the annual rainfall was only about seven or eight inches) while I fidgeted about inside. Once one of the Mexican families invited us to a *baile* which would begin, we were assured, at 8:00 o'clock, *estilo Americano* — that is, on time. Despite all my protestations Papa would not budge until finally around 10:00 the *mozo* returned to say that he had seen some people moving around the *sala*. Papa was still reluctant, but I insisted, and so we went, only to find that the hosts had had a dinner party for a few friends. These were the people the *mozo* had seen. The family was very polite and insisted on our having coffee or something, and we sat there a whole hour, miserably conscious of our *faux pas*, before the other guests began to arrive.

Having begun so late, the parties naturally lasted into the wee small hours, and there we ran up against Papa's firm conviction that the proper hour for breakfast was 8:00 A.M., and woe to anyone who straggled in later. He did it himself, since he took me to every dance. Just the same it was hard to be bright and cheery on two hours sleep, and I really appreciated the siesta hour.

Mama and Papa had very strong ties with the Germans, and she especially wanted me to marry a German, and she was inclined to push me in that direction. Once we went to a wedding in Monterrey — her idea being that I should meet two brothers living there, Germans, who were supposed to be very rich, handsome and altogether eligible. We made the wedding all right, but then were called home because one of the younger children was sick. So I never got to meet the so-desirable brothers.

But it wouldn't have mattered anyway. Because by that time I was in love with one of the two young Canadians, Dr. William Jamieson. He was a native of Ottawa, son of a druggist, and a graduate of McGill University. He had been practicing medicine in Oklahoma, then Indian Territory, and his old friend Tom Fairbairn had urged him to come to Torreón.

Billee had arrived in Torreón fortuitously on a day when all the doctors in town were busy with some kind of banquet or meeting where the wine was flowing freely. Clarita Carothers, wife of the American Consul, a witty and attractive woman, was walking down the street hunting for a doctor for her husband, George, who was very ill with a sore throat. She met Billee on the street and asked, "Aren't you Dr. Jamieson?"

When he nodded she asked bluntly, "Are you drunk?"

"I don't think so," he replied, and she took him by the arm to her house to see her husband. Billee cured up the sore throat, which was not diphtheria, as she had feared, and his practice was off to a good start. He soon made a lot of friends, being a witty and gregarious person.

Clara Carothers was in a sense the social arbiter among the younger group. She had a beautiful white skin, curly ash-blond hair and, in those days before mascara and eyebrow pencil, very pale lashes and brows. She used to say, "I have a face like an unbaked pie." George was a big man, who loved his food. One noon Billee ran into him just as he was going to have his lunch and he asked George to come and have a bite too. George declined. The party the night before had been a big one and he was too hungover to eat a thing.

"Well, anyway, come sit with me while I eat. Have a cup of coffee, at least," Billee urged.

When they were seated at the table in the restaurant George said, "Well, I might just have a bite. Nothing much. Waiter! Bring me two dozen oysters on the half shell."

Billee and I were engaged by the time I was nineteen. Papa thought I was too young, and I suppose Mama was still hoping that a dashing young German would come along. At any rate, they asked us to wait a year, and we did, Billee climbing the eighty-one steps up to the house every single night.

Billee was blond, with very blue eyes, and wore a blond

beard. During our engagement, however, he took a trip to San Antonio and came back clean shaven. It was quite a shock, and it took me a little time to get used to it.

The biggest social period of the year was just before Christmas when they held the *posadas.* Among the lower classes this was a religious affair, held every night for nine nights, during which a procession in which Mary and Joseph were impersonated, went from house to house asking for shelter and being turned away until the very last. With the upper crust it had turned into a series of dances, very elaborate affairs with several families acting as hosts for each. The ninth and final night the town bachelors played host. It made for a strenuous period, but it was an awful lot of fun.

Mama and Papa were among the hosts for one of the balls at the theater that year that I was engaged to Billee. A young Mexican couple, a doctor and his wife, also hosts, asked to be allowed to furnish the wines as their contribution. The bartenders were slow in setting up the bar that night, and several guests who had arrived early were impatient, one in particular, a man who had been out of town and who had come directly to the party without eating dinner. He asked for cognac, so Papa had them open up the case of cognac and, being a good host, took a glass of it himself, although he didn't care for it. After a sip or two he turned to Uncle Nep, who was back in business as a wine merchant, and said, "Taste this. I think there's something wrong with it."

Nep tasted it and said, "Tell them not to serve any more."

By that time the man who had no dinner was dying and several others were sick. Women screamed as they hunted for husbands or brothers. A Mexican man got up on a chair and yelled that the gringos were trying to kill off the Mexicans, and two brothers went to the heavily laden refreshment table and began stuffing food into handkerchiefs or napkins.

Papa was awfully ill, and Mama said, "I'll take Papa home. You try to find Dr. Neuman."

We couldn't find him, so Billee and I went home, but in the meantime a train had pulled in and we had to crawl between the cars, me with my train looped over my arm.

All the doctors in town were busy that night, and everyone of them except Billee diagnosed it as morphine poisoning and kept the patients walking and drinking black coffee. Billee said it was aconite and he gave Papa an enormous injection of something and wouldn't let him lift his head from the pillow — Papa had no desire to because every time he did he passed out. The laboratory in Mexico City confirmed Billee's diagnosis.

It was thought that the young doctor who had furnished the wines had done it, trying to get rid of his father-in-law, with whom he was on very bad terms. On the face of it, it was not too unreasonable a supposition, since a doctor would be able to get aconite more readily than a lot of other people. The young doctor was actually tried and sentenced to a year in jail, as was the porter who had carried the cognac to the place. But, actually, it seemed absurd that a man of the doctor's intelligence — and he was a very brilliant man — would have laid such a trail to himself and risked poisoning a lot of other people. Either the authorities recognized this or received some other information, because before the year was up he was pardoned and left the country.

Hindsight suggests that the poisoning attempt may have been a part of the ferment that finally led to the Revolution, a premature try at getting rid of a lot of wealthy and important people.

During this period we had moved from the old house on Viesca Street, where we had lived so many years, to the Chalet Wulff. In recognition of my status as a young woman I was given a set of bedroom furniture in bird's-eye maple, the most beautiful thing I'd ever seen, I thought.

Bullfighting had reached Torreón too. I was invited, along with a lot of other young girls, to be a queen at one of the bullfights. We were dressed in our best with *mantillas* over our heads, and we rode all around the town in beautiful equipages loaned by the wealthy Mexican families. But the bullfight was too much — I got sick and had to leave. And I never saw another one.

Chapter XIV — MARRIAGE

W BILLEE AND I were married April 5, 1906, in San Antonio at the home of Tante Carrie and Uncle Conrad. It was a very nice wedding with lots of relatives on hand and several people who had come up from Torreón for the occasion. I still have the menu of the supper that was served. We went to Mexico City on our honeymoon and then back to Torreón.

The town had grown so that they even had a modern apartment building, two stories high. Billee and I moved into this advanced structure, feeling that we were in the very van of civilization, almost on a par with New York or Chicago. Actually it really was very much ahead of time, for the apartments, even the upstairs ones, all had patios — a forerunner of the penthouse garden.

We were in the left apartment upstairs, and just across from us was Herr Quack. He was engaged, and his bride was coming from Germany with plenty of furniture and household goods, but in order to get this so-desirable apartment he had had to buy the previous tenant's furniture. Under us were four bachelors who were living it up, with a Chinese cook to take care of them. And on the other side were the Aery's. He was the undertaker, and she had just come back from the States, all agog with the new vogue for Japanese things. Their apartment was a welter of teacups, kimonos, obis, etc. They even had a large Japanese parasol, open, suspended over their bed.

One night Billee and I went to a dance in Lerdo. On the

way home it began to rain, to pour, as it sometimes does in the desert. By the time the *coche* reached our door the water was a foot deep, well over the sidewalk, and Billee had to take off his shoes and sox, roll up his trousers and carry me to the door, while he returned to pay the *cochero* and retrieve his shoes and sox. The electric lights, as usual, had vanished with the first stroke of lightning, and the hall was pitch black. I felt my way up the stairs and just as I reached the top a sepulchral voice came out of the blackness: "*Guten abend, Frau Doktor.*"

I nearly jumped out of my skin. When I peered around I made out poor Herr Quack, huddled in our doorway with a blanket around him. The rain, it appeared, had gone through his side of the roof like a clown through a paper hoop, leaving a foot of water in his apartment. Then it had soaked through the floor and inundated the Aery's abode, and they had been forced to retreat to the bed with only the Japanese parasol for protection.

Fortunately our side of the building hadn't been affected, so our things were all right. We took Herr Quack in for the night. However, the apartment had a water tank on top, which was supposed to be turned on to fill every day and then turned off. Despite the fact that there were seven or eight men living in the place, it always turned out to be my job to turn the thing off, lest the water spill over into our patio, so when our year's lease was up we moved. This time we got a brand-new house with our own well. But the well never developed any water, and we had to buy ours from the vendors who came by daily, two great lard buckets hung from a pole over their shoulders. When that lease was up we found a very nice house right across from the plaza.

The phone was in the *zaguán* or entrance hall, and most of the servants were afraid of it. I kept pointing out to them that the phone must be answered — it was a doctor's phone and it might mean life or death for someone, but they were still reluctant to touch it. Once we came home from somewhere and found María, the cook, backed up against the opposite wall of the *zaguán*, frantically telling the ringing phone, "But I tell you, he's not here." Death in the abstract did not affect the servants, perhaps because they saw too many concrete examples all around them all the time. Besides, who could tell what might happen if one touched that shrilling box on the wall?

We had the floors repainted in that house, and instead of doing one or two rooms at a time, they did the whole place. There were boards providing a path throughout for us to walk on during the four or five days it took the paint to dry. One night when Billee was out the phone rang and I started out on those boards to answer it. Halfway along, the lights went out, and there I was, stranded on a six-inch causeway in a sea of paint. I don't recall now whether the lights came back on or what, but I still remember the feeling of utter helplessness I had.

I liked being married, being on my own, and I found, as Mama had, that any really fancy cooking I had to do myself. Otherwise it was a very pleasant easy life. During the day I embroidered or sewed, and the women played bridge, the original bridge. We asked politely, "Partner, may I bridge it?" and Partner said, sweetly, "Pray do."

We had a bridge club that met once a week at someone's house, lunching first. (If you could call it lunch, since the big meal came in the middle of the day, and the ladies served accordingly.) One day we arrived at Clarita Carothers' house to find that she had completely forgotten that it was her turn to have us. But it didn't bother her. She just laughed and said, "Come on in. We can play while Juana fixes lunch."

That was all right with us, and we trooped in, all except Mrs. K., who was stout and very German.

Clarita repeated, "Really it's all right. Juana will have the meal ready in a few minutes."

Mrs. K. shook her head. "But you haf not cleaned the house."

Although there were more goods to be bought in the stores, the traveling salesmen (we called them drummers) still found Torreón a fertile field. One man took orders for custom-made shirts, and every man of substance in town ordered some. Once a man came through selling bolts of linen, which all the women hastened to purchase, because most of our clothes were made at home, and there was a dearth of good material. I bought a bolt, rejoicing in its fine quality for about the first two meters — then it suddenly turned into the coarsest sort of cotton, woven right onto the linen.

Billee's practice had grown, and his Spanish was now equal to dealing with most of his patients, but he found that often the more ignorant either had no idea what the doctor was trying to do or didn't care. Once he prescribed a certain medicine for a sick child — one teaspoonful three times a day. Next day they called him back frantically — the child was much worse. He probed about, trying to find the reason for the worsening of the child's condition. Finally he asked, "Did you give him the medicine?"

"Oh, yes, doctor, just the way you told us, three teaspoonsful four times a day."

There were other problems too with other nationalities. A certain German couple lived nearby, both extremely homely people. (Someone remarked uncharitably that it was just as well that they had taken each other out of circulation.) She had had three children with a midwife in attendance, but during the fourth pregnancy something went wrong and the midwife called in Billee. He was at the woman's bedside the better part of two days, neglecting his other patients in order to pull her through. Her husband had been away on a business trip during all this, but when he returned, instead of thanking Billee for saving his wife's life, he passed him on the street and cut him dead!

Billee went up to him. "Look here, what do you mean by refusing to speak to me? Don't you know I saved your wife's life?"

The man said stiffly, "I haf no wife. She is your wife."

"My wife! What the dickens are you talking about?"

"You haf looked upon her. She is no longer my wife. She is your wife," the German repeated stubbornly.

Billee had a wonderful sense of humor, and his eyes were twinkling when he asked, "Have you ever seen my wife?"

"Yes, I have seen Frau Jamieson. She is a very beautiful lady."

"Well, then," Billee demanded, "what the devil do you think I'd want with your wife?"

Even though the town had grown, we usually walked wherever we were going because everyone lived close by. We went calling often, to see someone just back from the States or abroad, to meet the newest visitors, to repay calls that had been made on us. Only occasionally, such as when we went to visit someone at a distance, did we take a *coche*. It's a funny thing, but I don't remember ever seeing a new *coche*. They were always dilapidated to the same degree, the horses in the same state of half-starved exhaustion. Why the *coches* didn't fall apart or the horses die . . . Someone did tell me a story about seeing two nuns in a *coche* somewhere. The floor of the thing gave way and the nuns fell through, but luckily on their feet. They had to run to keep up, for the *cochero* could not, over the rattle of the carriage and the hoofbeats of the horse, understand their cries. He thought they wanted him to go faster.

At first I had only one servant, a diminutive creature named Luz, who had two children, a girl of thirteen and a baby. The girl used to come and help her mother and got so she could wait on table very nicely. Luz became very fond of us and one day announced that she wanted to give us one of her children as a present. I might have taken the little girl, but when she offered me the baby I had to decline. I was pregnant myself.

Pregnancy in those days meant that you were confined to the house from the time you began to show even a little. There were no maternity clothes, you just let out your old things, but I did have a pongee coat, about three-quarter length, which I wore. My social life was confined to my family but there were still plenty of them, for the San Antonio relatives continued to come and go and some of Billee's family came to visit too. Things are certainly better now for pregnant women — better care and more freedom, but now and then when I see a woman, seven or eight months along, in shorts, I wonder whether it wouldn't be better if the rules were tightened up again some.

In Mexico babies had to be registered by the time they were eleven days old and on the afternoon of the 11th day we still hadn't decided on a name. Billee came rushing in and when he found that Mama and I had come to no conclusions he wrote the names (we were down to eight by that time) on slips of paper, put them in a hat, and made Mama draw one. Just as he went out the door I realized what I really wanted to name her, but it was too late. She was named Evelyn.

She was a good healthy baby except for what we called colic . I nursed her — as everyone did in those days — and I seemed to have plenty of milk, but she howled for six months. Finally Billee suggested I take her to a doctor in San Antonio, and I was quite willing because I'd lost twenty pounds and was completely exhausted after being up all night every night (the servants slept out). In those days they didn't weigh the babies all the time or we might have discovered sooner that she was simply hungry — my milk evidently lacked nourishment. From the minute we put her on the bottle, as the doctor suggested, she stopped crying and throve. She had such red cheeks that a strange woman came up to me in the park in San Antonio and berated me for painting a baby's face!

We lived a pleasant easy life, but tragedy was always close. Sometimes it was merely financial, and we would lose a friend or acquaintance, but more often it was worse. I danced with an attractive young Mexican at a *baile* — the next day he developed smallpox and a day later he was dead. Sometimes we managed to avert it. One night Mrs. Bonnett came rushing over to our house in her nightgown (the phone, as usual, was out of order) to get Billee — her baby had diphtheria and was choking to death. He rushed over in his pajamas, and since he had no instruments with him, he took a chicken feather, slid it down the child's thoat and saved its life.

He told me about a doctor who had been one of the honor graduates in his class at McGill. The man had come to Mexico, had taken to the bottle and finally wound up somewhere out in the sticks, still drinking, living in a miserable *jacal*, but taking good care of the extremely poor people who lived around there. Since they would ordinarily have had no care at all, they idolized him, and once, when he was jailed for drunkenness, his patients gathered up their pitiful little *centavos* (so hardly come by) and paid his fine. He died while delivering a baby. An early day Dr. Schweitzer, except for the liquor.

Chapter XV — REVOLUTION

W PORFIRIO DIAZ had been one of the heroes of the fight against Maximilian, a devout follower of Juárez. He was elected president in 1877, and one of the planks in his platform had been No Re-election, but the constitution had been amended twice to allow him to continue in office, and he was actually president until 1911. He was a strong president and did a great deal of good for Mexico, building up its prestige among the nations, establishing order and welcoming foreigners and foreign capital.

His solution to the everlasting problem of banditry was ingenious and successful. He was said to have called in all the top-flight bandits, given them uniforms and authority, and made them into a sort of national police force. They were known as *rurales* and were efficient and ruthless. An old mining man who spent years in Mexico told me the following story, supposed to be illustrative of their methods. Several *rurales* were on the track of some bandits who had fled into the mountains of Sonora, which is Yaqui country. The captain of the *rurales* went to one of the Yaquis, known as the best tracker in the area, and paid him to trail the bandits. But they found the men settled in a solid adobe hut which commanded the entrance to an *arroyo*, and it was evident that they could not be taken without considerable bloodshed. The Yaqui was asked to go talk to the bandits and persuade them to surrender. He succeeded and returned with the men, saying, "I promised that if they laid down their arms you would give them a fair trial."

"Certainly," said the captain and turned to the bandits, "Now, you've been tried, convicted and sentenced to be shot."

And they were, on the spot.

The *rurales* operated mostly in the country. Nearly every town had its own municipal government and *cuartel* of soldiers who served as police. The municipal government paid most of its attention to the wants and problems of the rich and the foreigners, just as the national government did. By the early 1900's the Díaz government had become very corrupt. The communal lands of the Indians had been taken away, and 96.6% of the land was in the hands of less than a thousand families. The Terrazas family, for example, owned most of the State of Chihuahua, Mexico's largest state. All these wealthy people were educated and charming and, on a strictly personal basis, generous, but they seemed to have no idea just how poor the rest of the population was.

In 1908 Díaz indicated that he would have no objection to some opposition at the polls, and Francisco Madero initiated a political crusade in which he condemned presidential succession and demanded effective suffrage. He was nominated by the anti-re-electionists, but was arrested for sedition in June, 1910. Escaping to Texas, he issued a statement which, in addition to political reforms, included a demand for agrarian reforms. This plank caught the ear of the downtrodden masses, who promptly gave him their support. Díaz attempted unsuccessfully to put down the resultant revolution and finally resigned in May, 1911, and left Mexico.

Just how well a lot of the masses understood Madero's platform is a moot point. Certainly it promised a change, and since most of them were already at the bottom of the economic heap, the only way to go was up. Plenty of them were pretty vague about the whole business. One man, asked by Billee what he was fighting for, said that he thought it was for one Don Luis (probably referring to Madero's Plan of

San Luis Potosi). Another was more cynical, "Let's see what's in it for me." Above all, I suspect, it promised excitement, change, something more interesting than the daily scramble to get enough to eat. To be issued a gun and ammunition, to travel around, to be paid (sometimes) to take out your frustrations by shooting and looting, to be somebody when you have been less than nobody. It had plenty of appeal, aside from the agrarian reforms.

Of course, all this business had been boiling for some time, but I had paid little attention. Women didn't in those days, and I was young and thoroughly engrossed with my two babies and a very comfortable life. Besides, it was unthinkable that things should change very much even if Francisco Madero were president. I knew him, he was the son of Don Evaristo, Papa's old friend, and the Maderos were not only among the 1,000 families, but were related to most of the rest of them.

The foreigners were almost entirely on Díaz's side. He had welcomed them, to begin with, the order was established, things should be allowed to go on as they were. Of course, the majority of the people were desperately poor, but surely something could be done about that without going to war. Madero was an idealist and a zealot, and he appealed to the rabble. Some men felt that the Federal troops would make short work of the rebels; others were not so sure — the rabble was awfully numerous.

That first year of the Revolution we stayed on in Torreón, moving up first to the big house with Mama and Papa and then later to a small house that Papa owned at the foot of the hill next to his office. It was then that Barrie, my second baby, became very ill with colitis. She had been a seven-months baby and had never been very strong, and now she lay in a coma for many days. When a group of American doctors came through Torreón for some reason, Billee persuaded them to

The Federals try out handmade cannons in the streets

Federal troops occupied Torreón at the beginning of the Mexican Revolution in 1910. Here they barricade Calle Viesca with sandbags.

Federal troops at the entrance to Chalet Wulff during the 1910 uprising. Papa's office is seen at right.

Federal soldiers posed for their picture in the garden of the Wulff home.

look at her, and a change of treatment was prescribed. But she died. Six weeks later Evelyn had double pneumonia. Nowadays pneumonia is easier to cure than the common cold but then all we had to treat her with was cloths wrung out of cold water wrapped around her chest and covered with pieces of flannel. Fortunately she pulled through.

All this obscured my view of the Revolution, although Papa and Billee were most concerned, since the fighting was increasing and it seemed inevitable that Torreón, with its command of the rail lines, should be involved sooner or later. Other foreigners were getting alarmed, and there was a constant stream of people leaving for the United States and elsewhere. The Continental Rubber Co., evacuated all its employees. The town was full of soldiers, who wore the white shirts and pants and helmets and, naturally, the crossed ammunition belts. The officers were resplendent in their uniforms. These were Federal troops — I don't think I actually saw any of the rebels at this time. *Puestos* sprang up at the foot of the hill to serve the soldiers; a barber set up his chair on the sidewalk in front of Papa's office, and one had to wade through a foot of hair to pass. Papa dared not say anything though, because the winds of change had reached Torreón, whether the fighting had or not, and the peons were a lot less subservient than they had been.

Early in the spring of 1911 Billee brought me and the baby to San Antonio, where I stayed at the Hutchins Hotel, but he returned by the next train, for he was now a doctor for the Red Cross. Thereafter for several months I tried to cope with loneliness and sorrow and anxiety, although the San Antonio relatives were most kind and thoughtful, and I did get occasional letters from Mexico.

Federal troops had arrived in Torreón to supplement the ones already there, and when it appeared, from the capture of Gómez Palacio and Lerdo, that an attack on Torreón was imminent, barricades were set up in the streets and preparations for battle made. From the windows of the Chalet Wulff it was possible with field glasses to see a great horde of people, just waiting. These were civilians, not soldiers, who had come from as far away as Zacatecas in order to loot Torreón when the town was taken. Mama, packing to leave, saw them. She caught the last train out of town, and it was nearly a month before Papa knew that she had arrived safely in San Antonio.

A letter of Billee's, written to his father in Ottawa and published in one of the Canadian papers, gave a good account of his efforts to get back to Torreón and the battle that took place. It is dated May 24, 1911.

> Dear Dad:
>
> Well, I have just passed through my first experience of actual warfare and can't say that I am stuck on it. On and after this date, when I want more warfare, I shall seek the M.P. show. Any bloodthirsty tendencies of atavistic descent or origin have been totally annihilated.
>
> On the 21st of April I took Dalla and the kiddo to San Antonio. We were held up about 100 kilometers out of Torreón but allowed to pass, as some eighty members of the Madero families, that is, servants and children, were on the train going to Monterrey. After we left the rebels burned the bridge behind us and the station also. We arrived in Eagle Pass too late for the S.P. connection and had to lay over for 24 hours in that little hole. Arrived in S. A. Sunday night and started for here on Tuesday morning. On arriving at Spofford, the conductor told me that there was no train for Torreón so I hiked back to S. A.
>
> After hanging around there for 8 days, I started south by way of Laredo. After leaving Saltillo, we were held up and $350 taken from the express car, but the passengers were not molested; in fact many of us knew nothing of the rebels until the following morning when we awoke some 75 kilometers farther on, where we stayed for 10 hours on account of a

burnt bridge. The rebels destroyed the telegraph lines, so that we had to feel our way to San Luis Potosi, where we found the northbound train waiting.

They had relieved the engineer and conductor of their watches and the peon said that they had showed a gun against his (the peon's) belly and had taken a dollar away from him. Furthermore they were waiting for our train to treat us the same way.

As soon as this news got around the passengers were unanimous about going back to San Luis. The conductor of the train was an Englishman and spoke very little Spanish, and as I was the only one on board who could speak both languages, the rest requested me to beseech the conductor to return. The telegraph, or rather telephone lines, being open to San Luis, the agent got communication with that place and had a wire sent by way of Queretaro to Aguascalientes asking for orders. Finally, they came and we went back, arriving in San Luis at 8:15 p.m.

Next morning we started out again and arrived in Aguas without incident. Waited there for 8 hours and took the northbound train on the Central, arriving in Torreón the next day at 12 noon.

It took me 125 hours for a journey that ordinarily is done in 23 hours.

Those on the train leaving Laredo the day following us did not get home for a week.

When I arrived everything was excitement. The rebels had possession of Gómez Palacio, 5 kilometers away, and were preparing to attack Torreón.

On Thursday morning, 11th, the last train out left Torreón with some 25 foreigners on board, mostly women, including Mrs. Wulff. Until this morning we did not know if they had arrived in San Antonio or not. At 2 p.m. the same day a private train loaded with wealthy Mexicans and their families left for the south, but was turned back at the first station out. That afternoon there was a short skirmish which lasted about an hour. Saturday morning at 10 a.m. the ball opened in earnest. The firing commenced east of the city, around the

Continental rubber plant and the smelter, the Alameda and the Chinese gardens. Then all along the river bank it became alive with rebels.

The rattle of musketry was intermingled with the crash of the metralladora (machine gun) and the cries of the contesting parties.

Viva Madero and *Viva Porfirio Díaz* were heard on all sides. All day long the firing was an almost continuous crash. Bullets whistled up and down the streets. I was in the emergency hospital in the centre of town (Garza Aldape's drugstore). Presently the wounded began to come in. The first man was a *pelado* (lower class Mexican) who, while crossing Morelos Avenue, was shot twice through the right leg, breaking the tibia in four places. The next one was a curious man who stuck his head out from the corner of the street to see what was going on. He found out, but the information did him no good, for a Mauser bullet went through his brain. All day long we worked, and when night came we had to wait, as the rebels took the electric light plant on the edge of town and shut off the current.

We did not dare to stir, for the Federals were firing at every shadow. They fired constantly at the Red Cross, although they had promised to respect it. All night we sat in the drugstore, Drs. Gerkins, Lim, Garza Aldape and I, besides the stretcher bearers and young Carlos Gonzalez, who had volunteered for the Red Cross work. The mosquitoes, the heat, and the cries of the wounded whom we were unable to send to the hospital, made it a night of distress for all. Early next morning I started out to hunt some breakfast. The firing had ceased about 3 a.m., but I had not gone more than a block when the whine of two Mauser bullets which passed close to me made me reconsider my determination to break my fast, and I returned muy damn pronto to the hospital to chew the cud of reflection and meditate on the horrible way in which war interferes with a man's digestion or rather his getting something to digest. The cud of reflection proving a poor substitute for ham, eggs, and coffee, Garza Aldape, Gerkins, Carlitos Gonzalez and I started forth at 6 a. m., again seeking refreshment, and also to put Carlitos under the protection of the U. S. Consulate, as both he and his father had taken a very prominent part against the rebel forces in the Laguna. Garza Aldape was going home, as he had not seen his family for 24 hours and was anxious. He lives near the Alameda, which was the very centre of the firing. He left Gerkins and me at the corner of Rodriguez and Morelos, and I watched him to go the bend in the street at Acuña street. Then he suddenly wheeled around and came back on the run, saying, "*Muchas balas.*" The battle had opened up again.

Somehow or other he got home, but he couldn't get back again. I worked until 11 a.m. Sunday, then went to bed until 5 p.m. All Saturday night we could hear the rebels yelling, "*Viva Madero*" and "*Muera Porfirio Díaz.*" Every time they yelled the machine gun would spit forth its hail in the direction of the sound. A thunderstorm about midnight made the sounds more distinct, and it seemed as if the firing was in the next street.

Sunday night I retired about 12, and about 2 a. m. I heard the march past of the Federals as they evacuated the town. Their ammunition had given out. Either through accident or design the last consignment of cartridges was found to be worthless, having wooden maneuver bullets instead of steel. General Lojero then and there made the mistake of his life. Instead of surrendering the town, he determined to evacuate, thus leaving the town at the mercy of the populace. The Federal fire ceased about 4 a.m., it having been kept up by a few *rurales* and volunteers while the troops were evacuating. At 5:30 a. m., the rebels sent scouts out, who reported that the town was empty of soldiers. Soon we could hear the yells of the people and the rebels as they entered.

The mob entered the Chinese Bank Building and on the third floor found a number of newly arrived Chinamen whom they threw out of the windows to the street and their friends below finished them.

Little children were stood up against the wall and shot down, crying "*No me maten*" (Don't kill me). Chinese women were served the same way. Mounted troopers rode to the outskirts of the town and dragged Chinamen in to the plaza by the hair to execution. Some took refuge in the

Casino, the fine $250,000 club of the city. The mob entered and after killing them sacked the place, leaving it an utter ruin. I saw one fellow with a fine heavy silk plush curtain which he was using for a saddle blanket.

For three hours the slaughter of Chinese and the sacking of buildings went on, until the arrival of Castro and Emilio Madero, brother of Francisco, put an end to the most savage display ever seen or heard of in a supposedly civilized country. The rebels meanwhile had burnt the *presidencia* (city hall), the jail, the store of Henry Wulff (Dalla's uncle), Alfonso Campbell's place next door, after sacking them.

All the pawnshops were sacked, as well as the Chinese steam laundry and the stores kept by Arabs. Some Spanish stores also suffered, notably that of Victorero Bros., who lost everything. The plate glass windows of the Suiza and Harzer building next door were shot to pieces. The house of Carlos Gonzalez was looted of everything and the elegant bedrooms and parlors are now used as a stable for rebel troopers. On Monday afternoon three or four men came to Mr. Wulff's house and demanded arms.

I had moved my furniture to the little house beside Mr. Wulff's and they wanted to know who lived there. They were told *"un doctor de la Cruz Roja."* After talking this over for a few minutes one of them turned and asked, *"Donde anda este doctor rojo?"* (Where is this red doctor?)

It was explained to them with some difficulty that I wore a Red Cross on my arm and was a physician in charge of a hospital. With that they seemed to be satisfied and left. Four times that afternoon came parties to search for arms, but offered no molestation. The last bunch asked who lived there, and the servant girl told him, "Don Federico Wulff."

He immediately became more respectful and said, "He is a great friend of the Maderos, isn't he?" "Yes", said the cook and he departed. Mr. Wulff was a great friend of old Don Evaristo Madero, and Dalla, when she was 15 years old, took a trip all over California with him and his two daughters.

Then began the burial of the dead. They were loaded into carts and taken to the cemetery, where the Mexicans were buried in trenches inside and the Chinese outside. I was out to the cemetery a few days later attending the burial of James McCarty, superintendent of railroads in Torreón, who was found dead in bed. In one trench were probably 25 cheap coffins containing dead, left uncovered. One fellow had been thrown there without a coffin and lay half propped up against the side of the grave.

Then came the tidings of peace. Everybody was joyful; the church bells rang for an hour; pistols and guns were shot off. But I don't think that the rank and file of the rebels were any too glad, as they will be disarmed and sent back to work. These fellows have been getting a peso a day for fighting, have had a good horse and rifle, and they are going to be very sore over giving them up. The first thing that was done was to send a force of 250 men to the ranches to protect the workmen and *hacendados* while the crop was being harvested. As already little bands have been pillaging, this is very necessary. At El Porvenir a force of rebels was passing the other day while 10 yards away 8 or 10 men were robbing the store. The proprietor was there with a gun against his "tummy" and you can bet your last frijol that he wasn't very talkative.

Last Thursday or Friday the lower classes gave a *"baile"* (dance) in the Chinese Laundry, where the previous Monday they had slaughtered all the inmates.

The first train from the U. S. came in yesterday morn and was followed by one from Mexico City, bearing mail detained for two weeks.

Well, I reckon this is enough for one time. During this diverting episode I have about lost track of time. Love to all.

Will.

Billee managed to miss recounting one very interesting episode in his letter. Across from the house of the tailor, Mr. Lindquist, who was also the Swedish Consul, was a Chinese restaurant where some fourteen or sixteen Chinese were employed. When word came of the killing of the Chinese, Mrs. Lindquist brought the restaurant employees into her house and hid them. At her door she placed a table with a pretty little Mexican servant girl and some beer and sweets of various kinds. Half a dozen times during the three hours that the massacre lasted, rebels came to demand the Chinese. Each time Mrs. Lindquist refused, insisting that they wait till the "*comandante*" arrived. After the killing was stopped, the surviving Chinese were to be taken to the *cuartel* for safety, and Billee, to his dismay, found himself leading them across town. It was a nervous procedure, for tempers were still hot, and one cross look or something equally trivial could have started things all over again. Mrs. Lindquist was later decorated by the Chinese government. Some twelve or fifteen years later Billee was in Chicago on business when he heard someone calling his name. It was one of these Chinese, and he took Billee to a fine restaurant he owned and wined and dined him enthusiastically.

The first group of rebels who came to search the big house demanded all the guns Papa had, and he produced them all, except one pistol, which he had thrown down the trash chute, (This chute ran from the top of the house to the basement, with an opening on every floor, and was crammed with papers and trash, since there had been no *mozo* to empty it for some time.) One soldier stuck a gun in Papa's side and, showing a pistol he had found, said, "Don't you dare tell the others that I have this." The others kept insisting that there must be another pistol, but with the gun pointed at him Papa could only reiterate that they had them all. Finally Atilana, the cook, spoke up, "If Mr. Wulff says you have them all, you must have them, because he's an honorable man and speaks the truth. So if you are missing a gun, one of you must have it." The guilty one then collapsed, brought out the gun and they all left. But they had gone through Papa's office and warehouse and made him open every box of instruments and tools. Another group took Fidi's horse, a very fine one, and, finding the saddle from Bub's horse, which we had sold recently, kept insisting that there must be a horse to go with the saddle.

During the looting Billee ran across a peon wearing a silk hat and carrying a commode, on which he was beating with a stick. He asked the man what he had, but he didn't know, and when Billee explained, he threw it away in disgust.

When Emilio Madero arrived in Torreón and stopped the killing of the Chinese, he also ordered the looting stopped "on pain of death," so then people began bringing back the things they had stolen. A dry irrigation ditch was filled with typewriters and other things that had been taken.

In midsummer Billee sold what was left of his practice to his cousin, Dr. Harmon Cole, and came to the United States. We went from San Antonio to Chicago, where he took a brush-up course in some field of medicine, and came to El Paso, where we settled down and have remained ever since. But Mexico was still with us, not only because El Paso is just across the river from Juárez, Mexico, but also because Mama and Papa stayed down in Torreón, coming up to El Paso when things got too hot and then returning. Papa owned about four city blocks in the middle of town, the house, the office and various other properties, which he had to keep an eye on and eventually dispose of, and his brothers also owned property there. Besides, it had been their home for twenty-five years.

Chapter XVI — REFUGEE TRAIN

W FRANCISCO MADERO became President, but he was neither a strong man nor a practical politician. One of the casualties of his regime was the promised agrarian reform, which angered and alienated many of his followers. Huerta, who had been in Torreón at the beginning of the Revolution, succeeded him, and Madero was assassinated three years later while in "protective custody." Some of the generals and lesser officers, reluctant to give up their power, kept the war going, while others, under the guise of patriotism, took to banditry. Huerta was no more to the generals' taste than Madero and, more important, he did not suit the United States. Presidents came and went. Some were strong men, some were not, and some were in office too briefly to tell one way or the other. (One man is supposed to have been president for forty-five minutes.) But Mexico is a big country, and the events of Mexico City had less impact on the northern part than might have been expected. The one continuing fact of life in northern Mexico was Pancho Villa.

By September of 1913 Torreón had been under siege by some sort of ISTAS, probably real *villistas*, for four months. It was a desultory sort of thing, and the inhabitants of the town were in far more danger of dying of boredom than anything else, their only amusement being the daily trip to the railroad station to see if by any chance a train might be coming in. There was no mail, no news except rumor. They were reduced for food to the basics — *tortillas* and beans and coffee, and sometimes one or more of these was temporarily lacking.

Then came word that Villa was really going to try to take Torreón. Papa and nine others, including Ed and Tosca, took refuge in the basement of the big house with its thick rock walls. Atilana, the cook, remained upstairs in the kitchen, saying that she wasn't afraid if only they would stuff a mattress in the window. Downstairs there were only two narrow entrances and they put mattresses and springs in those and stayed there, listening to the gunfire. Villa had placed machine guns, which sounded, Papa said, like worn-out sewing machines, on the top of the hill and shot over the house at the town below. Luckily Papa had laid in a supply of food, so that when at the end of ten days the siege was lifted, they were merely sleepy and tired. The Federal garrison announced that the road was clear to Monterrey and Laredo, and the United States decided to run a train out of Torreón to take out all foreigners. Villa apparently was willing, except that he stipulated that no Spaniards be allowed on the train. He hated the Spaniards for some reason, but whether this was a permanent emotion or merely a thing of the moment, I have no idea.

Papa and Mr. Cunard Cummings, the British Vice Consul, were in charge, since twenty-eight British Sisters of the Sacred Heart were to board the train in Gómez Palacio, their convent having been looted and burned. Papa was named American Consular Agent for the train, which had been already arranged for and provisioned by the Consular Agent in Torreón, Mr. Carothers. He had provided a lot of canned goods and a two-burner oil stove for the 350 passengers. Papa was given 500 pesos for expenses for the twelve-hour trip, the scheduled time to Monterrey, where American Consul General Philip Hanna was in overall command. The trip finally cost 5,000 pesos and took thirteen *days*.

This is the story of that trip as Papa told it:

The train was composed of a lot of box cars (some, supposed to contain firewood for the engine, turned out to be empties), several first class and second class passenger cars, a diminutive Pullman which was said to have bedbugs, one engine with very bad flues, a tender, and a combination car used as diningroom, kitchen, warehouse and, last but not least, an arena in which the race, hunger and other riots took place (except when they were going on in the aisles of the Pullman). There were also two cars used for the sick — one woman was just getting over scarlet fever. I used one of these cars myself to stay out of the way of the chronic complainers. But even there I was not always safe, and now and then one of these gripers got booted off the train. Unfortunately the train proceeded so slowly that there was no chance of losing any of them permanently.

I had gotten a taste of this before the train ever started when a group of the righteous came to me to suggest that an American carpenter, who was known as a drinker if not a drunk, be left behind in Torreón. I managed to hold my temper and remind them that I was supposed to take out all foreigners regardless of their personal habits. Another problem was posed when a close friend of mine, a Spaniard, came to me and begged to be taken on the train, as Villa had set a price on his head. I had to refuse him, but did remark that, of course, if he should happen to get on the train without my knowledge . . . He did and stayed hidden behind the trunks for some days.

The crew consisted of an able Mexican conductor, Mr. Rubalcaba, who was later shot by Villa, a Negro engineer, a train boss who never had a chance to exercise his function, Pullman porters, and, supposedly, some car cleaners. These last never materialized at all.

The train departed on the afternoon of Sept. 25, 1913, and proceeded majestically one mile to the border of the state of Durango on the Nazas, where the cook exploded the two burner oil stove when he tried to cook the first meal for us. There was no harm done except that it took all the water on the train to put out the fire. At Gomez, a few miles farther on, the nuns boarded the train and, learning the situation, offered their wood stove. This was put on the platform of the combination car, but it threatened to set the car on fire and the walls around it had to be constantly watered to prevent this. The final solution was to fall back on the ever useful frijoles and coffee and meat, when we could get it, cooked in large tubs over open fires on the ground. If an emergency arose the tubs could be put on the platforms. The canned goods provided were being saved for the sick and for a real emergency, but they soon started vanishing, and a guard had to be set over them. We also searched the passengers' luggage, and the most indignant were, naturally, those who had the most cans hidden in their bags.

We managed to do 40 miles that first afternoon, and at San Pedro we received the encouraging news that several bridges ahead had been burnt. We sent a wire to Torreón, calling for a work train and materials, also for some car cleaners for the sanitation of the train, now stopped no one knew for how long. It was necessary to provide about half a steer daily to feed the passengers, although some of them did go to a small hotel in the town. On the 26th the work train arrived and behind it a military train, which simply commandeered it and took it to the front. It did return, however, along with some of the materials. In the meantime the refugee train, without water for the toilets, had to be shifted a train's length to clean up the first position and then back again to clean up the second. The gripers, now in full cry, objected loudly, and I appointed the noisiest one Sanitary Inspector.

The train carried 3 flags, British, American, and a white one. There having been no wood for the engine we had to pick up ties along the way. Once we found a car full of wood and appropriated that, later paying for it, which delighted the owner, as he had given the thing up for lost.

In San Pedro we directed a polite communication to the Maderista General Isabel Robles, who controlled that part of the state, advising him of our coming and asking for his assistance. But some of the men passengers, whom I consulted, didn't want to wait for his reply, so we moved along to the first burnt bridge, which we repaired by putting in new ties, since the girders were still in place. After crossing we dismantled the bridge, so that neither of the contending parties could accuse us of aiding the enemy.

The drunken carpenter, having overimbibed in San Pedro, came to to find that the train had gone off without him. He got a hand car and followed, knowing that the train progressed very slowly — in fact, it stopped at nearly every rancho. He was caught by a rebel band, headed by Cabecilla Cortinas, who were hiding in the brush planning to attack the train, which they suspected of carrying Federals. The carpenter explained matters, and Cortinas promised to shoot him if he were lying. The train passengers had in the meantime repaired and dismantled another bridge and stopped for the night at Palomas. Cortinas and his band came next morning, with the carpenter, and ordered us to return to San Pedro. He also wanted to take our engine, but finally settled for a handcar. I hoped that the righteous who had wanted to leave the carpenter behind were aware that he had probably saved all our lives. Not only that, but as a direct result of his unfortunate habits.

Mr. Cummings and I went to meet Gen. Robles on a handcar with a white flag. The general was very polite but said that since he had destroyed the road ahead it would be impossible for the train to go on. He advised us to return to San Pedro and assemble a mule and wagon caravan and said he would give us all possible help. So we returned to San Pedro, again rebuilding and dismantling the same two bridges.

In San Pedro we rented a lot of mules, Studebaker wagons, and carriages for the sick, putting seats in the wagons and bed-springs in the coaches. I talked to Mr. Carothers on the phone and learned that Villa had finally really taken Torreón. While I was talking two soldiers came along and demolished the phone box with axes. I was only too happy that they had confined themselves to the box. Then I got a message from a friend, saying that when the news of the surrender of Torreón reached San Pedro the federal garrison and all civil authorities of San Pedro had fled and that the rabble were preparing to attack the train. I ordered steam up and then got a message from another friend, saying that they had intercepted a message from Villa ordering his men to blow up the train, hoping that the United States would then intervene.

Mr. Cummings and I then called a meeting of all the men passengers to help us decide what to do. One of the men remarked that as long as they were to be killed, they might as well be killed near home. Amazingly, no one else objected to this idiotic suggestion or had anything constructive to offer. I gave up on the democratic process right then and decided to go on, but to take a sidetrack south to the Hacienda de Hornos, feeling that the attackers, on foot, could hardly do much to the train in motion. Two reliable passengers were placed on each platform to stand guard for the night.

The train was always stopping for one reason or another, sometimes for no reason at all, and I would have to go up front to see what the trouble was. One of the troubles with the engine, outside of its original deficiencies, was the muddy water we had to use in the boiler. Once the train stopped in the middle of the night and when I got off, using a little ladder I had made for myself, it suddenly started up again and left me behind. Luckily I could see the lights of a rancho ahead and knew it would stop there, so I ran and finally caught up with it. Although some of the passengers had brought along luggage — some even trunks — I had brought none for so short a journey, and my boots were getting very thin.

No attack was attempted that night, but about dawn along came 11 military trains over the supposedly torn up road — evidently they had repaired it. These trains, commanded by Generals Ocarranza and Aubert, were said to have had with them several millions of pesos for the Torreón banks, a great amount of provisions, and 3,000 new Federal soldiers to relieve the town. On hearing that Torreón had fallen they immediately doubled back for Monterrey. It seemed that this would be a wonderful pilot train for us, but remembering what Robles had said, I was careful to give them 8 hours' start. In 2 hours, however, we had caught up — the trains, which occupied about a half mile in length, were bailing

water into their tanks, and we did likewise. Then we followed to the Laguna de Mayran, where the military engineers
discovered that 8 of their 11 engines were "dead." (But no
one dared tell the generals so.) One of the generals, it was
said, paid his soldiers a bottle of beer a day — judging by the
number of empties we saw along the right of way, this was
probably true.

I wanted to pass the trains on a siding, but the generals
would not permit it, so we waited. During this period a child
was born on the train and named Minerva for the station
close by, and another died. I passed up the funeral to find
a mudhole in which to cool my aching feet.

The Federal troops which had evacuated Torreón and a
great number of fleeing civilians were on the road back of us,
and the generals were sending back some of their equipment
to pick up these unfortunates. Over our protests that it
would not do for a neutral train to pick up Federal soldiers
and sympathizers, we were ordered to send back an engine
and a flatcar to pick up some of the artillery which the Federals had abandoned in the fields they themselves had flood-
ed around Torreón. When the engine and flatcar returned
they were so thickly covered with people that not even a
piece of metal could be seen, and we couldn't get them off
until I had the engineer start backing up as if to return to
Torreón. In five minutes the people were gone.

While we were there the wife and daughters of my friend,
the Spaniard who had hidden on the train, arrived early one
morning in their nightclothes on horseback, having heard
that Villa was going to attack their ranch, and begged to be
taken on the train. In the shadow of the Federal trains I
felt I could safely comply.

We had endless conferences with the generals, and each
time either Cummings or I or both of us would have to take
a handcar to go up to the front of the train. It was probably
this that caused me to lose 20 pounds on that trip.

General Bravo, one of the Federal generals who had fled
Torreón, was a fine old man of 75 and a personal friend of
Mr. Cummings. He and some others had fled into the moun-
tains, where they were without food for several days. We de-

This refugee train carried foreigners from besieged Torreón in 1913. Passengers were obliged to pile out and repair burnt-out bridges in order to cross.

This wagon train, organized to evacuate civilians, was never used.

These Maderistas rounded up all arms owned by civilians in Torreón at the onset of the Revolution.

Victoriano Huerta shown here was one of the Federal officers in Torreón at the start of the Revolution.

In the background is the cuartel where survivors of the Chinese massacre were taken for safe keeping.

cided to send some food to him and fixed up a small basket, but the problem was to get it there, since we were both too exhausted to walk and our boots were worn out. However, we saw a white spot in the darkness, which turned out to be a horse. We had found a rebel soldier hidden in the wood car who had a saddle and by threatening to expose him to the Federals we managed to borrow it. It had no bridle and only one stirrup, but Cummings managed to mount it and with a stick to prod the beast along, went off into the night. He was elected for this mission, not only because the general was his friend, but because he had had the forethought to bring a pair of bedroom slippers.

Afraid to continue to stay behind the Federal trains, I was able to exchange my handcar for one belonging to a railroad man who was with the Federal trains and sent a message to Monterrey, asking the consul general to send a relief train to Hipolito, to which place we intended to walk, carrying our sick and whatever else we could handle.

Suddenly seven water tank cars appeared, the Federals took on water and started up again. The refugee train followed and we arrived in Hipolito the same night. We tried to wire Monterrey to hold the relief train, but the wires were down, and it was said that some bridges ahead had been burnt. So then we tried negotiating with the engineer of an engine capable of pulling our train upgrade to Saltillo, but the Federals held the engine and the engineer. Then we decided to leave for Monterrey, but we had no fuel. The generals agreed to help us get some coal, but there was none available. But I saw a car loaded with new ties and had the engineer hook onto it, as if by mistake, and we started off and on the way we met the relief train, under the command of Dr. Ryan. We were ecstatic over the delicacies it carried, such as butter and oranges.

Instead of 500 pesos and 12 hours, as planned, the trip had taken 13 days and cost 5,000 pesos, which we had had to borrow along the way. I was too tired to continue on to Laredo, but the Sisters of the Sacred Heart did, staying on the train for 10 days longer without ever reaching their destination.

I went to Tampico, where some of the other refugees and I got a Norwegian oil tanker bound for New Orleans. The Borgestad could not carry passengers, so we were signed on as crew, the ladies as stewardesses, and we received 25¢ for our services. The real crew treated us royally, giving up their cabins to us.

We all carried a letter from the American Consul in Tampico to the American Red Cross representative in New Orleans, with instructions to give us our railroad fare to our homes in the states. With this Red Cross representative I had the only really disagreeable dealings on the entire trip. We waited all morning, and the man finally condescended to see us in the afternoon about 30 minutes, so he said, before the departure of the train on which he intended to send the 'Texas cattle', as he called us. He insisted on our signing pauper certificates, to which I objected on the ground that we were not paupers, but refugees — in fact, we all had a little money, which we would be needing at our destinations. To one woman who had $8.00 he offered $3.00 to complete the purchase of a ticket to Houston. I finally left in disgust and reported the whole matter to Monterrey. Later I found that due to the stand I had taken the Red Cross man had finally given them all they asked for, but whether with or without the pauper certificates I did not discover. The man who told me this had managed to get 3 tickets for Los Angeles, 2 extra ones for his 2 sons whom he intended to pick up in San Antonio. He generously offered me one of the tickets to San Antonio and I accepted, but insisted on paying for his pullman.

Actually I had a draft for $250 from Consul Hanna, but no one would cash it for me, owing to my looks and dress, and I finally had to wire my brother in law in San Antonio for funds. When I arrived in San Antonio I found that Fidi was being married in Brady the next day. I had known nothing of the marriage since there had been no mail or wires for so long. I wired Mama, who was with Dalla in El Paso, and we managed to arrive in Brady after the ceremony had already begun.

Once, before they fled, Papa and Mama hid the silver. There was a built-in seat in the entry hall, and he broke open the bottom of that and buried the silver. Later on when they returned they discovered that the silver had been disturbed, but was still all there. Atilana said that there had been a rumor that the house was to be sacked, so she and some other old servants of ours had taken everything out of the house and hidden it in their own little houses and then put it back. Which may or may not be true, but things seemed to bear out the story.

Chapter XVII — MORE REVOLUTION

ὧ THE REVOLUTION went on for ten years. Papa and Mama stayed down there, Harry also for a number of years, and Bub was there too for awhile. They came up to El Paso when things got too rough and we would put mattresses on the floor, but once they stayed long enough to rent a little house in El Paso. In the meantime we had occasional tastes of the fighting right across the Rio Grande from El Paso. You could stand on the roof of the Paso Del Norte Hotel and watch the battles. Once, in fact, when Billee was up there a bullet passed him so closely that he felt the breeze, and there is a story, which may or may not be true, that in one of the battles more people (two) were killed on the American side than in Juárez.

Torreón was taken and retaken, and each general coming in issued his own paper money, so that anything you had left over from the previous regime was worthless. It got so that people, when they heard a change was in the offing, rushed down to buy whatever they could with the old money. Once Harry had to take a lot of ladies' kid gloves — that was all there was. Much more stable than the generals' currency was scrip issued by various companies. At the time of the refugee train they were using scrip printed on parchment by the House of Purcell. Later on, a man named William Weeks issued notes to pay his employees, and these were used so extensively that the name "bilimbique" (an attempt at the man's name) was used for all paper money in that area.

Services lagged; equipment was old and needed repair, and the spirit of independence which had permeated the workers of the country, while healthy, was apt to be misdirected. The Coahuila Pacific Railroad had always been an uncertain quantity, so much so that it had been nicknamed the *Cuando Puede* (when it can). During the Revolution Bub had occasion to take it and noted that they had a lengthy and previously unscheduled stop at some *rancho*. He discovered that the engineer had a great friend there with whom he played checkers — each time the train passed he stopped for a game.

I don't know who was President in 1915. At any rate, things were so quiet that they were having racing in Juárez. We went one afternoon and found ourselves seated in a box right next to Villa. He looked just as his pictures had shown him, and he was very jovial, obviously enjoying himself. But his reputation was so bloodthirsty even then that Evelyn, who was about eight, exclaimed, "Why, he hasn't even shot anybody yet!"

We decided to take a trip down to Torreón to see Mama and Papa and also the Potters at Tlahualilo. Billee couldn't go, but Alice went with me and we took Evelyn along.

At that time there was only one Pullman on the train between Juárez and Mexico City that was reputedly free of bedbugs, so Papa wired us when that car came through Torreón and we hastened to board it next day in Juárez. Despite this we took cans of insect powder along. The porter was a rat-faced Mexican, an unsavory creature who scared Evelyn half to death by peeking into her berth when she was getting ready for bed. He tried the same thing on Alice and she really bawled him out in Spanish, so next morning he was more sullen than before. Luckily we reached our destination very early, because when he started making up the berths the insect powder we had scattered around rose in clouds and he had a severe choking spell. If looks could have killed, we'd have been dead.

We got off at some little station, short of Torreón, and were met by the Potters and taken to the hacienda where we spent about two weeks very pleasantly. We played golf, and the pet deer, Clarita, followed us about and sometimes nipped at our rear ends when we were putting. Incidentally, it had been badly misnamed, for it developed enormous antlers and during the rutting season was so fierce that it had to be confined behind a wire fence. There was tea every afternoon and dinner parties at night, and it was good to see old friends from Gómez and Torreón again. Everyone was very optimistic about peace. Evelyn and the cook's little girl, Chata, became bosom friends, and I hired a man to accompany them when they went riding every afternoon on burros. What I didn't know was that the ground covered on these rides grew shorter every day while the man spent more and more time in one of the *cantinas* in Zaragosa, the nearby town, and the children waited patiently outside. There was a canal full of stagnant water close by, and one day Chata's burro wandered into it and started to roll over. Chata screamed, and the man, just emerging from the saloon, sent a little boy about ten years old to bring her out. He managed this without trouble, but when he was sent after Evelyn she was so much larger that they both fell into the smelly green water.

When it came time to take the train to Torreón I realized that Mexico had a long way to go to catch up. There was one first-class car on the train, but that was full, so the three of us sat in a boxcar, which had two boards nailed along the walls to provide seats. It seemed all right, for the car was practically empty and the trip took only about an hour. The grim reminder was the soldiers riding on the roof of each car, complete with rifles and ammunition belts. However, the train stopped at every little station along the way and more and more people got on, including four drunken soldiers and their weapons, and the atmosphere grew less pleasant with every mile. The passengers were not supposed to carry livestock, but one little old woman got on and suddenly darted over and shoved a basket under my feet. The smell and the peeping emanating from it suggested chickens, and I could just see myself trying to disclaim ownership.

Torreón looked very sad, with bullet holes in the walls, and other buildings in ruins. The big house was intact — as a matter of fact, it was hit only twice in all those ten years of war, once when a shell knocked down one of the balcony pillars and another time when a bullet went through one of the windows and hit the wall opposite. Which, considering that the attackers usually chose to shoot over the house at the town, is certainly a record of some kind. (Perhaps the fact that it was rented for some years to the American Consulate had something to do with it.)

Mama and Papa were reasonably well and delighted to see us. Food was a trifle on the short side, but one thing, Mama said, was that they could get plenty of lovely fresh eggs. A little old woman brought them six a week, and certainly she would step up the order now that we were there. But, surprisingly, the woman refused.

"Why not?" Mama asked. "I'd even be glad to pay you a little premium."

The woman shook her head sadly. "I can't, señora."

"Why not?"

"Because I have only one chicken."

We had a nice visit with them and Evelyn was fascinated with the Chalet Wulff with its big rooms and the balconies off each one. When it was time to go to the train I forgot my golf bag. Papa, finding it, sent the woman who cleaned his office after me with the bag. But since she worked for him only one day a week and the rest of the time was a professional beggar, the first policeman she encountered arrested her for theft. By the time that was straightened out the train had gone, and he had to ship the bag to me in El Paso.

We were dismayed to find the same rat-faced porter on the Pullman. He gave us dirty looks and we were distinctly nervous, but nothing happened.

The Revolution picked up again after that. Villa was still around. He would take Torreón and each businessman was supposed to fork up a certain amount of money. Once Papa was away, and Harry and Triny, who were acting as his agents, heard it announced at the theater that Papa's share would be 30,000 pesos, an impossible sum. So they hopped on the train for Veracruz and stayed away till things died down.

The first time that Villa took the town he settled down in a big house in front of the plaza, with two bands playing night and day in front. He assessed all the businessmen and he impressed Harmon Cole into taking care of all his sick and wounded. Then he asked Harmon for a bill. Harmon charged him something like 1,500 pesos, and everyone laughed at him. Did he expect to get paid when Villa had already levied forced loans on every halfway solvent man in town? But, much to their surprise and Harmon's too, probably, Villa's second in command appeared with a paper sack full of money and paid him exactly what he had asked for. Harmon became a friend of Villa's after that. He said that much later he asked Villa just why he had staged that raid on Columbus, New Mexico, and Villa replied that he hadn't intended to raid the town, that he had simply been after an American to whom he had given some thousands of pesos to buy arms and ammunition and who had not done so.

Villa was hated and adored, and his men obeyed him implicitly. Robert McCart, Alice's husband, was a mining engineer who spent some time down in Mexico. Once when he took a trip down there he found that the pass Villa had given him was instantly honored everywhere in Villa's territory, while his Federal pass invariably let him in for much questioning and delay as he went from one general's bailiwick to another.

When the AS&R decided to abandon the mine that Rob was managing for them in Mexico, one of the New York bigwigs came down to help him close up the place. They filled the Cadillac roadster Rob had with portable property and finally had to tie things on the back. Rob suggested to the man that while they were going over the big lava bed that lay in their path it would be well for him to sit on the back of the car and hold onto things, as the going would undoubtedly be rough. The man, who was on the grumpy side, acquiesced silently and they started out. When they were halfway across the lava bed Rob called out to him that it wouldn't be too long now, but the man did not reply and Rob decided that he was simply being his usual surly self. When they reached the end of the lava bed, Rob called back that in a minute the man could climb inside. Still no reply. He turned around, and sure enough the man was gone. Rob turned around and went back and found the man wearily stumbling along over the lava. This time the man was grumpy, but not silent.

For years the story circulated in Mexico that Villa's death had been arranged for by the government, that they had simply looked around for someone who hated Villa enough to do the deed. The man chosen had been a storekeeper at a mine Rob was managing. Villa had raided the place and demolished the store, and the man had nursed a deep and abiding hate for Villa from then on. The man was jailed after the assassination but, so the story goes, when Hipolito Villa, brother of Pancho, began giving the government trouble, the assassin was released, presumably as a threat to Hipolito. Whether or not this is true, I do know that the man came to

Juárez about that time and called Rob and asked for his help in getting his wife and daughter across into the United States. He himself, being a convicted criminal, could not enter, and I never heard what happened to him.

There used to be in Juárez a street musician, fat, dirty and jolly, who played an instrument of his own design, which he called a *girafono*. It consisted of a cow's horn, with a mouth organ set into the curve and on top the two halves of a bicycle bell and the back of a small alarm clock. He would play anything requested, from Mexican music to the Artillery Song and the Anvil Chorus, blowing on the mouth organ, tapping the horn and the bells on top with a knitting needle or a thimble. Once, when we were listening to him, a newspaper woman got all excited about the idea of getting the man into the states for the night-club circuit. The bartender called us over and whispered that the man couldn't enter the U. S., as he had been one of those who did the tortures for Villa.

There were other stories about the Revolution, some of them very funny. During one of the more peaceful times one of the women at Tlahualilo decided to entertain the rest of the colony at dinner. She had an enormous turkey just ready for the oven when word came from the next ranch that the rebels were on the way. Everyone at Tlahualilo always kept a bag packed, ready for flight, so they got ready to drive over to Hornos where they could take the train. At the last moment the hostess decided it would be a shame to leave that nice, fat turkey, so she bundled it into a basket and took it along. It was a nuisance in the carriage, which was full enough as it was, and at Hornos it was a problem to carry the big basket onto the train. It was wintertime, but the train was hot, so she bribed the porter to keep all the windows of the Pullman open so the turkey wouldn't spoil. The other passengers, half frozen, complained bitterly, but all the porter would say was, "*No se puede.*" (It can't be done.)

At Eagle Pass, where they had to change trains, the basket broke and the woman paid a man to go get a big box for the turkey. There was some trouble at the customs too, but finally they arrived at the St. Anthony Hotel in San Antonio, and she had to pay to have the fowl put into the hotel refrigerator. She shared a room with Mrs. Vaughn, and in the middle of the night they were awakened by a knocking on the door. It was some agents of the American government who had come to arrest them on a charge of bringing a wild turkey into the United States in violation of the wild-life treaty between the two governments. It took some time to persuade the men it was a domestic fowl, raised at the *hacienda*. Then after that the woman had to drive some fifteen miles in a carriage to the little town where her mother lived, still carrying the turkey which by now was almost literally worth its weight in gold. When she reached home she told her little sister, who had come out to greet them, "Tell Mama not to worry, I have a turkey ready for the oven." The little girl danced into the house but returned almost immediately to say, "Mama says she doesn't need it — she's got one in the oven right now."

Papa had had to go to Mexico City on business and he was having dinner with some friends there when word came that the last train north was about to leave. He had to get on it, for he was building a dam near Torreón, so his friends bundled him into a *coche* and, as an afterthought, thrust the remains of the turkey they had eaten into his suitcase, knowing that he would probably be able to get nothing on the train. The train was so full that he couldn't get in the door of the Pullman, so someone opened a window and his friends literally pushed Papa through, along with the suitcase. The car was jampacked, so he had to upend the suitcase and sit on it in the aisle. At the other end of the car an American woman whom he knew kept making signs to him, finally spelling out on her fingers in deaf and dumb language that they were getting off soon and if he could work his way up to that end he could have her seat. It took him an unconscionable time but finally he did manage to get her seat when she left, but there was not room enough to open the suitcase to get at the turkey.

Supposedly the Revolution was for the poor people, but bureaucracy still flourished, as it always had, for the rich and important. One summer afternoon a very poor Mexican woman came to Papa for help. One of her children had died and, according to Mexican law, had to be buried before sundown. She had been sitting in the *presidencia* trying to get a burial permit since early morning, totally ignored while the clerks took care of better-heeled customers. Now it was almost 6 o'clock and she still had no permit. Papa sent her in a *coche* back to the *presidencia* with a note from him to get the permit and then onto the cemetery with the little coffin. Later on Canuta (don't you just love Mexican names?) came to work for him. She was a happy-go-lucky person, always willing and pleasant and a fine cook. She had half a dozen illegitimate children, born of different fathers, who were taken care of by Jesús María, who was eleven. Jesús María was a sad child — Papa said he never saw her smile but once, when he brought her a doll from the States.

Canuta was very enterprising. Among other things she used to sneak Papa's electric iron out in her *rebozo* and rent it out to her neighbors. He gave her a little plot of ground and the *vigas* (roof timbers) from Uncle Henry's ruined store, and she built herself a little house. When he gave her Mama's old sewing machine she went into business as a seamstrees, charging fifty *centavos* a garment.

At some time during the later years of the Revolution Papa sold the big house to a man who had been a bootblack, I think, and had made a fortune out of the Revolution. He sold the whole works, furniture, glassware, china and all. Later the man asked Papa to come up to the house to show him which wine glasses went with which wines. Papa was ushered into the parlor where Mama's French furniture, maroon velvet, curly gilt legs and all, still stood. Tethered to the leg of the big sofa was a *chivito* (kid).

The man, incidentally, was later arrested on some charge and given a long sentence. But he was given two cells, one of which he fitted out as an office, and he continued to transact business and, presumably, make money. He even had a secretary.

In 1916 came the Pershing Expedition into Mexico, and El Paso was really full of soldiers. There were tent cities in which the 50,000 men were quartered, and the streetcars running to Fort Bliss went tandem, and there were plenty of beaux for all the young ladies in town. The Hotel Paso del Norte, recently completed, blossomed out with *the dansants* (it was the Castle period). Alice was a young lady then, and she had more than her share of the young officers trailing after her. Once she went with a young officer to a carnival where he won a live rooster, which he offered to her. Since we were then living in an apartment she refused it and suggested they leave the struggling creature behind, but he wouldn't hear of it. He tucked it under his arm, carefully concealed by the dashing cape he wore, and they went to the *dansant* at the Del Norte. But the rooster was still alive and squawking, so they finally went up on the mezzanine floor and tucked it into a dark corner under one of the chairs. In case the hotel has been wondering about that fowl all these years, this is the explanation.

El Paso was full of refugees too, mainly wealthy, who had fled Villa. Ironically, part of them were members of or related to the Madero family.

Chapter XVIII — EPILOGUE

ᴕ MAMA DIDN'T LIVE to enjoy the peace, for she died in 1921 and is buried here in El Paso. Papa went back to Torreón but he built no more dams. The rolling cylinders he used to use, which had come from Germany, were a casualty of World War I. Furthermore, legislation passed in Mexico made such work almost prohibitive. For instance, one of the laws stated that if you hired someone on contract, you had to pay him three months' severance pay whether he ever worked a lick or not. On this last job Papa, who over the years had acquired a working knowledge of Mexican law equal to that of any lawyer's, got around that by hiring each one of his two or three hundred workers each morning on a day's contract and paying off at night. It involved a tremendous amount of bookkeeping but was the only way he could do it.

During the 30's Papa got sick and decided to come to El Paso. He was feeling so ill that he dared not travel alone, so he brought along the little Mexican girl who was working for him then. She was a nice child, but we had to cook all her meals for her, as she had never seen a gas stove. She stayed in El Paso for about three or four days, but we were so busy with taking Papa for tests and trying to cope with our other houseguest, Sandy, that we never had a chance to show the little maid even El Paso's downtown section. Our Negro cook, Estelle, did take the poor child to a New Year's Eve celebration at her house, which must have been interesting, as Estelle spoke no Spanish, and the girl no English.

We did take her to the cemetery when we went out to put some flowers on Mama's grave, and she was quite impressed, although it was midwinter and the place was hardly at its best. When we took her to Juárez to put her on the train the inspecter slashed the clean blue and white quilt in which she had her worldly goods all over with purple crayon.

Evelyn went back to visit in Torreón and Tlahualilo in 1927 or '28 and found that the town had grown considerably. It even had one paved street, a long avenue with a parkway down the middle. At each intersection was a statue. Some of the statuary was heroic, some patriotic, and some frankly amatory, including a statue of two nudes curved into an intense embrace. A holiday of some kind came along, and someone conceived the idea of putting little Mexican flags into the hands of the various statues, including the lovers. It was the thing for the young people to drive their cars every afternoon up and down the avenue, and General Escobar, who headed the Torreón garrison, also used to drive up and down. A year or two later he started his own revolution, but that, luckily, didn't last very long.

During the 30's Papa finally finished selling off what was left of his and his brothers' property and came to live in El Paso. He rented a little house near us and even bought a car and learned to drive. This was very nice for us, since he seldom used it and had no objection to our doing so. But as he never got over fifteen miles per hour he was a menace to traffic even then, and we were glad when he got rid of it. Eventually he left El Paso and went back to San Antonio to live with Triny in a little house on S. Presa Street. But in 1945 he came to El Paso for a visit and, although he was getting very deaf, he was still spry enough to insist on carrying his own suitcases. Four years later he died, aged 93, with all his own teeth.

Of our immediate family only Alice and Robert and I remain but the Chalet Wulff still stands on the hill at Torreón. For a time, I understand, it was used as an army barracks, but it is now empty, though still solid, dignified and impressive — last tangible evidence of a life now gone forever. But the flavor, diluted by time and events, still lingers.